THE [SECRET]S OF PLANNING
A PROFITABLE BUSINESS

- **Products and services:** What kind of business do I want?
- **People:** Who and how many customers do I estimate will use my services or buy my products?
- **Place:** Is the proposed space in my home adaptable to business?
- **Price:** What should I charge?
- **Protection:** Do I need insurance, copyright or patent?
- **Promotion:** What will be the methods of marketing and advertising?
- **Persistence:** Do I have what it takes—the drive to work hard with optimism?
- **Problems of success:** Have I anticipated the new challenges that any start-up business faces when the public says yes, Yes, YES!

For the answers, look to *Homebased Businesses!*

HOMEBASED BUSINESSES

Beverly Neuer Feldman, Ed. D.

FAWCETT CREST • NEW YORK

Library of Congress Catalog Card Number: 83-50903

ISBN 0-449-21810-4

This edition published by arrangement with Till Press

Manufactured in the United States of America

First Ballantine Books Edition: January 1990

Kahn, Harold S

Because of Tillie, Felicia, Kathleen, and Susan

DPL Phil Rel & Ø 374.9 R629j
DPL Bus. & F.N. 658 S8660
DPL Phil.Rel. & ED 374.91 G358F
DPL Bus. & F.N. 651. H396H
DPL Bus & F.N 658 K1210

DPL Gen INFO 670.5 B6459
DPL Art & Lit 806.51 K129W

Contents in Brief

Contents

Souvenirs, Special Events, Sperm Donor, Stationery, Stonecutter, Telephone Services, Toy Library, Trade-In Presents, Underwear, Video, Vineyards, Wholesale Catalogs, Wigs, Wild West, Wine, Wood Carving, Writing, Yellow Pages

Services from A to Z

Accountant, Advertising Consultant or Representative, Adviser, After-Hours Rescue, Agent/Agency, Animal Care, Airplane Rides, Anthropologist, Antiques, Appraiser, Aquariums, Arbitrageur, Architect, Art, Astrologist, Auctioneer, Auto Doctor, Auto Researcher, Auto for Hire, Auto Sleuth, Bankbook Reconciler, Bartenders, Beauty Expert, Bibliotist, Birds, Bodyguards and Bouncers, Books, Bookkeeper, Broker, Business Instructor, Camp Adviser, Child Care, Childbirth Educator, Chimney Sweep, Clipping Service, Clubs, Club Discount, Collection Agency, Color Consultant, School for Color Consultants, Commodities Adviser, Computers, Computer Artist, Computer Consultant/Systems Analyst, Computer Home Parties, Computer Magazines/Books/Newsletters, Computer Operator, Computer Repair Technician, Computer School, Computer Software Writer, Consultant, Contractor, Convention Planner, Cooking Classes, Cosmetologist, Costumer, Counselor, Courier Service, Dating Service, Dog Trainer, Direct Mail Service, Education Consultant, Envelopes, Escort Agency, Exercise Studio, Expediter, Fashion Consultant, Fix-It, Folk Healer, Food Stylist, Fortune-Teller, Freight Traffic Consultant, Fund-Raiser, Funeral Director, Garage Sales, Gardener, Genealogist, Gift Selection Service, Gofer, Gophers, Grantmanship, Graphologist, Greetings, Guide, Headhunter, Health Services, Home Nursing Agency, Home Maintenance, Hotel/Motel Consultant, House Inspector, Humiliation Healer, Hypnotist, Image Consultant, Instruction, Interior Designer, Ironer, Learning Skills Center, Librarian, Limousine Service, Lost-and-Found Sleuth, Marriage, Mediator, Meeting Planner, Midwife, Model, Music, Needle Arts Instruction, Notary, Newspaper Distributor, Nutritionist, Party Planner, Party Server,

Piano Mover, Piano Tuner, Photographer, Picnic Pro, Plant Tender, Politics, P.O. Boxes, Promoter, Property Manager, Psychic, Public Relations, Relocation Agent, Remail Service, Rent-a-: Celebrity—Naturalist—Sheep—Suitcase—Tablecloth—Tool, Researcher, Restorer, Reunion Pro, Roommate-Finding Service, Secretary-Typist, Self-Defense, Seminars, Sewing Expert, Sex Therapist, Sitter, Shopper, Space Planner/Organizer, Soaps, Social Graces Instructor, Speech Pathologist, Spiritualist, Stockbroker, Storyteller, Super Sports, Swamp Meet, Telephone, Telephone Systems Analyst/Installer, Textbook Buybacks, Tour Leader, Travel Agent/Agencies, Transcriber, Translator, Trucker, Tutor, Typesetter, Washerwoman, Wedding Consultant, Widow Coach, Word Processor, Word Professional, Wrapping Service

Open the Door

If I am not for myself, who will be for me?
If I am only for myself, what am I?
And if not now—When?

                                       —Hillel

In looking back over the past in preparation for this book, I realized that I've been involved in homebased businesses for over thirty-five years. My first home earnings centered around a telephone, a bicycle, and leg muscles. In order to get a telephone, a scarce commodity and difficult to obtain during World War II, I became a Western Union "boy," opening a branch office (a breakfast table in a corner of our one-bedroom apartment) in a housing project. Western Union provided the telephone, a bicycle (at cost). I expanded the telegram service to include a fifty-cents-a-message center for people without telephones in our isolated community. I quit "Dad died need money for casket," "Married someone else cancel wedding tomorrow," "In jail need bond" just as soon as phones become easier to obtain.

Four years later, when housing and phones were not an issue, I opened our large, rambling English house to eight foster children, providing twenty-four-hour care seven days a week. It was hard, heartbreaking work at times. The children came, stayed until their families could regroup, left, and new children arrived. I earned more money than I could have at an outside job, was able to care for my own young child, and felt good about providing a much needed social service.

Other homebased businesses in my past: dog breeding, chicken farming (a disaster), telephone soliciting, teaching guitar, running a nursery school, making custom mobiles for infants, toy manufacturing, and selling by mail order.

Of that group, the business of toy manufacturer was a really big enterprise. My daughter designed a silly-looking yarn octopus, which hung from her canopied bed and evoked much enthusiastic comment from friends. She and I began to make these toys and one by one they sold. Then my husband decided to take samples to some local buying offices, and when he returned home with orders for 144 dozen, I was overwhelmed! How could we produce that number? Where could we store yarn and stock? Where would we get the money to buy the yarn?

How did we produce not only 144 dozen but hundreds of dozens as Octo-Puss caught on across the nation? By hiring one outside contractor and teaching her how to make them. She picked up the yarn and the specifications at our home, delivered the work to the home-workers she employed, and brought back the finished Octo-Pusses to us.

Where did we store the yarn and the stock? Our bedroom, of course. After a while, it seemed quite natural to have hundreds of those Octo-Pusses sharing our bedroom.

Where did we get the money to buy the yarn? From our friendly neighborhood banker. The face value of the orders for the original 144 dozen and our purchase plan of buying the yarn directly from the mill—increasing our margin of profit—convinced the banker to make the loan.

We developed a "line," small, medium, large, and giant sizes, in any color combination. Octo-Puss was a hot item for three years, and was featured in the Neiman Marcus Christmas catalog. It provided good newspaper copy because it was a teenager's creation. Japan knocked off the idea, sold it for less, and that was the end of "Octo-Puss." From that three-year experience I learned a great deal about production, marketing, and promotion, including anticipating unfair competition and the "here today, gone tomorrow" aspect of business.

DIVERSIFYING

Perhaps it was that unanticipated end of Octo-Puss that changed my career philosophy from having one enterprise at a time to several. After all, big business diversifies by buying up or into companies whose products are not necessarily related to the parent company. It is a common strategy for successful survival in a changing economy. Individuals can follow suit in a small way, *diversifying* their enterprises as well as *pyramiding* their assets.

Today, even the super Madison Avenue advertising agencies are changing their traditional operations. The soaring costs of advertising have forced them to find less expensive means to promote a client's product. They are buying established companies as well as forming subsidiaries that offer adjunct specialized services such as image consultants (see listing under Services), language translators for the ads, color consultants, and even match-cover designs.

Diversifying is a way for the parent companies to grow, either by offering new services or reinvesting in businesses other than their own. To trace a company's true ownership back through the web of subsidiaries takes a detective.

Think how you can apply your skills and energies to more than one income-producing business. If you are employed, what sideline business can be developed after hours and on days off? The business can be work-related or totally different. While servicing my refrigerator the repairman informed me that he also makes repairs on his *own* time and charges a great deal less than the major chain, his employer. An airplane pilot moonlights as a puppeteer for parties. A psychiatrist carves intricate pipes for profit and his own therapy. Another doctor loves to grow and collect cacti and each weekend sells the surplus stock at his garden stand in front of his house.

One couple started the nucleus of their business as relocation counselors. They had contacted several large corporations who were relocating their plants to one of the sunbelt cities and offered to find suitable housing for their employees. They met the executives at the airport, whisked them into a rented limousine, conducted a tour of the city, recommending neighborhoods, schools, temples and churches, shopping areas. This business took hold and now, because they returned to school to obtain real estate sales licenses, they are able to sell the property they show. They diversified their services to include a Homeowners Yellow Pages, charging carefully screened merchants, tradespeople, and professionals a fee to be listed. Word-of-mouth advertising has established their business quickly because they added the touches that make people exclaim and tell others.

Can you imagine coming into your new home to find the refrigerator stocked, flowers and candy on the coffee table, a delicious hot meal, the beds clean-sheeted and turned down, a piece of candy on the pillow. Even the local residents use their services to find an apartment or house. Makes one want to move.

PYRAMIDING

Just about all of us have experience in pyramiding our personal assets. Purchases of a refrigerator, car, sailboat, or second home increase our net worth. All of these "things" (perhaps acquired one by one) build up our financial standing. These things can be used as collateral for bank loans to provide start-up capital. Because "things" are bought with our earnings, it is important that some of us acquirers are able to increase our earnings, to realize the next dream of "I wish I had . . . or I wish I were able to . . ."

Daydreams about being richer need not remain daydreams. I have hung over many a kitchen sink doing many a dish and fretted about our economic state. It seemed we were the national debt. Economic good health can be achieved when you become multiskilled. Acquiring new skills on top of the ones you already have opens up new careers. Skills do not necessarily have to be related to one another. Your economic base will grow—upward bound as you grow, learning something new in preparation for another business adventure.

It is a nonstop process. I know. I have gone through this process, successfully.

From my experience with numerous homebased businesses, I feel entitled to a new degree, an H.B.B., after my name. Now most of my activities center around professional services. I am a homebased business/career/education consultant. This knowledge and expertise enables me to have a private consultant practice, to teach the subject at colleges and universities, to write books and articles, to appear on television and radio shows, and to conduct seminars. As side businesses, I sell and distribute another "hot" (like Octo-Puss was) jewelry item, an electronic flashing pin.

4

Plus, I operate a mail-order business, a publishing company, and I invest in classic cars.

For some home-workers it may take more than one business to provide enough cash; for others, working hard at one business may be enough of a payoff. For me, the money is pleasant, but it is the multi-projects that are the dynamite incentives.

Diversification suits my temperament. Boredom is not my work companion. Fresh energy is generated to such an extent that it surprises even me. Tune in to what makes you work happy, and increased productivity is a natural result. Big business in the U.S. has finally become aware of the connection between working happy and productivity—following Japan's leadership. To combat employees' work boredom and resulting loss of industriousness, corporations have developed Quality of Work Life programs, which include job rotating and teaching new skills to employees. And I've been doing that for years! Charlie Chaplin's classic movie bit, *Modern Times*, I believe, on a production line should have been a teaching film for industry years ago.

PARLAYING

"Parlay," says Webster's, means "to increase into something of much greater value." How can you miss if you *parlay your skills into a continuing self-development program*, thus opening new options? *The surest bet you can make is on yourself.*

For those who employ themselves, self-efficiency and self-sufficiency are the assets in beginning a business with little investment and keeping outside labor costs low. If you know you are going to be the bookkeeper and do not know the first thing about record-keeping, then go to school and take a beginner's class in bookkeeping, or get a bookkeeper to set up your books and instruct you how they should be kept, or buy a how-to book on the subject. Need to type your business correspondence and can't-as-yet-afford to hire a homebased typing service? Well, learn how to type. Or if salesmanship is essential to the success of your business, do not worry, choose from one of the many one-day seminars offered by college and university extension programs that deal with the skill or the information you want to learn. I've

5

attended many of them, even a few on the same subject I teach just to be sure I'm on top of the latest information and to compare content and style of the competition.

DIVERSIFY. PYRAMID. PARLAY.

Welcome Home

Then give the world the best you have
And the best will come back to you.
　　　　　　　—Madeline Bridges

Are you another Estee Lauder, Frank Lloyd Wright, Missoni, Paolo Soleri, Kathleen Whiteside Taylor? What do these people have in common? Home is where their business is or where it began. The first loaf of Pepperidge Farm bread was baked for family consumption, but the aroma traveled far and wide over the countryside to become a major national bakery. You may never have heard of the kitchen-table–conceived mail-order company Brookstone, but enough people did for it to bring a recent selling price of nine million dollars. We all know of one person who works from home—the President of the United States!

Billions of dollars are earned each year in the fast-growing underground economy of homebased businesses. Incomes have a wide variance. People whom I have interviewed earn from twenty-five dollars per week to over a million dollars per year. Some of the businesses provide the sole source of income; others, a second or third income.

We seem to have come full circle; just a couple of hundred years ago it was the custom for people to earn their living from their homes. Shops were set up in front rooms, in back of the house, in a shed, in a loft, a stable, an office attached to a house—anyplace at all where they could work, eat, and sleep under one roof. Men were the first to abandon home-work for factory jobs, leaving wives to carry on the "cottage industries." Women were the milliners, the dressmakers, the bakers, the confectioners, the grocers, the dry-goods merchants.

7

In 1856, *The Chamber's Journal of Popular Literature* (London) had this to say about "the trade" in a house:

> *In a certain street of a certain town there are three houses standing together and forming a remarkable exception from the general fate of the houses of that street which has been to yield one after another to the advancing genius of Commerce. Most have broken out into shops; some have put large brass plates on their doors, and declared themselves millinery establishments, little boards announcing Furnished Apartments, a chemist's shop— houses stuffed—O horrid word—with goods. The idea of any one of these houses condescending to any such useful purpose as that of—a shop. It would seem as if creation must henceforth have but half its brightness—resistance to trade is finite and the fate of all houses of gentility will be theirs—they must become shops.*

In time it became déclassé in this country to have a business in your home. It was a telltale sign that the person had not quite made it.

STATUS

Now homebased has become a status symbol. The number of publicized success stories of homebased businesses has added a kind of glamour, made it fashionable, and now denotes independence and a sense of mission accomplished. It even produces envy among those who are still on a nine-to-five treadmill. The grander entrepreneur is shown in magazine articles doing his or her typing by a swimming pool or better yet, floating on an inflated raft in the pool— just thinking up a new idea. This kind of hype entices others to join the quiet exodus from the marketplace to find a better work life; a return to the "old-fashioned" way people used to earn a living.

The fact that almost all Swiss watch parts are made by Highland families during the long winters between dairying seasons never lessened the status and impeccable reputation of Swiss watches.

FUTURIZING THE PRESENT

"People will work at home someday" says futurist Robert Theobald, British socioeconomist, contending that he's never "met a worse place to work than an office. . . . Computers will allow people to move back to rural areas if they so choose."

Another forecaster, oft-quoted author Alvin Toffler, calls the home of the future an "electronic cottage." He suggests that millions of us may soon spend our time home instead of going to an office or a factory. Companies now are encouraging their executives to work at home more than at their offices.

If indeed, according to government statistics, there are now twenty million home businesses, plus all those "underground" businesses undetected by the U.S. agencies, I'd say the future is here.

MAXIFLEX

Many of us home-workers enjoy shipping and "soaping," flexitiming, siesta-ing, and particularly the liberty and luxury of working between 8:00 p.m. and 6:00 a.m.

Now the government is incorporating some of the fringe benefits of working at home into their offices. The Department of Labor signed a "progressive" contract with its employees. Please note that any similarities of working conditions is purely nonaccidental. The new collective bargaining contract allows the employees:

- A nontraditional work schedule, "flexitime." There are several plans to choose from and the most liberal is known as "maxiflex." In "maxiflex," an employee's forty-hour work week can be concentrated into four days, between 6:00 a.m. and 8:00 p.m., with Mondays or Fridays off.
- The right to watch the soaps or play radios and cassettes while doing their tasks.

Companies are discontinuing piped-in music and are allowing workers the option of listening to their own radios.

In the research for this book, I thought of the homebased businesses I know as a consumer and they add up to a goodly number. I seek out homebased businesses because of their originality of product, informality, better quality, atmosphere, intimacy (I've always enjoyed shopping at Ma and Pa stores), easy parking, and a sense of discovery. So much time is spent obtaining goods and services, the process might as well be pleasurable.

A homebased business is not for the person who remarks, *"How can you stand being at home so much?"* For me it is a happier work life than when I commuted two hours each day to a well-paying, interesting job, attended endless meetings, and frankly, spent more time at the doctor's office.

HOMEBASED IS NOT HOUSE-BOUND.

Working Happy

Home is the place to do the things you want to do. Here we eat just when we want to. It's terrible to allow conventional habits to gain a hold on a whole household; to eat, sleep and live by clock ticks.

—Zelda Fitzgerald

QUALITY OF LIFE

Where else can you have a coffee cup in one hand, a telephone cradled to your ear, and transact a business deal in your bathrobe? And, instead of taking two breaks in an eight-hour, nine-to-five day, there are days when there are eight breaks in a two-hour workday. Where else can you pack an order while you stir the soup, pet the child, dog, and/or lover?

Home can be the center of all the action. It is a work haven where moods can be indulged, biorhythms heeded, and hail, sleet, and snow be damned! It's cozy. Remember, home is the place that was so good to come back to—after work, after a trip, after dinner and a show. Well, you can be there not only after, but before.

Working at home is viewed by some people as a superior way of spending one's life. With so many hours of the days and weeks devoted to earning our daily bread,* it may be a

*For an exact figure, multiply 8 (work hours per day) × 40 (hours per week) × 4½ (work weeks per month) × 11 (work months per year) × 40 (years of working life).

better idea for you to stay home to bake—remember Pepperidge Farm or Good Stuff breads.

THE BOSS FACTOR

Some of us need to be our own boss. Our credo is "One Who Hesitates Is Bossed!" We can realize the dream: "I am the President!"

Working overtime becomes the means to a chosen end, rather than a demonstration of your dedication to someone else's company. Your productivity can follow your own natural rhythms, rather than the dictates of someone else.

Common office requests often begin with "Would you mind . . . ?" Now you can answer "Yes, I do mind."

MOONLIGHTING

So common today, moonlighting is called the subterranean economy. A second job can be related to what you do in your regular work or can be totally unrelated. Interestingly, the number of men who moonlight has decreased, because of the increasing number of working wives and the trend toward smaller families. The Bureau of Labor Statistics figures show that the number of women who hold two jobs has doubled in the last ten years. Many determined women who are single providers for their children have jobs back to back in an attempt to make a livable wage and to provide food and shelter, medical care, education, and so on.

Many professions just do not provide an adequate financial return. Teaching is one of them. Many teachers moonlight. A math teacher wrote a book about how to teach school and make a living at the same time. He's into car washes and Christmas tree lots.

Workers with relatively flexible schedules, such as firefighters and police officers, go for the extra cash. An increasing number of professionals and managers are finding an after-five market for their skills.

One source of income just doesn't meet the bills these days. Ask your senator his or her fee for speaking engagements. Even with all their perks, they cry "poor." Congress had to put a dollar ceiling on their moonlighting.

Although the government cannot keep track of the millions of self-employed it is reported that nearly five million people held down two or more jobs in 1980.

Moonlighting has launched many businesses, but my advice to clients is *hang onto that job while testing the waters for your own business*. The salary checks can alleviate that sink-or-swim feeling, give the homebased business a chance to develop, and *feed the family*.

The reasons for moonlighting can be for other than cash. Diversion from what people do by day, or to test a career change, or for additional ego—food can be the motivating factor.

CAPITAL INVESTMENT

Because a homebased business can begin with little or no start-up capital, going into a venture can become a reality for small-time operators. Store and office rentals are prohibitive these days. Salaries and fringe benefits for employees have forced some still-new businesses to fold. Undercapitalization is a major cause for business failures.

A home business skirts these common "new-business" problems. Bed, bread, and boss under one roof allows more leeway time to develop the business and releases capital to flow into advertising and promotion. The low overhead of homebased business can mean that the owner draws a salary from the income much sooner and more easily than one can be drawn from other kinds of new businesses in their early days.

FAMILY LIFE

A child in a day-care center from 6:00 a.m. to 6:00 p.m.? Is this the best solution to the child-care problem for working parents? It is the only answer for many—weary, overextended parents picking up overly tired, cranky children.

Today only 7 percent of all family units fit the traditional model—a male who works outside the home, a housewife, and two teen-age children. Approximately 12 million workers, many of them women, hold part-time jobs. Part-time work by both men and women is growing steadily.

There are mothers and fathers who want to stay home with their children but who cannot make ends meet on one paycheck. The homemaker tries to find a home business that provides an income. Some of these endeavors develop into such a thriving business that the husband or wife eventually quits the outside job to join the home front.

It can strengthen the family unit. Husband and wife can work as a team or in different home businesses. There's time to take care of home crises—time to attend to children's needs.

Children see firsthand what it is their parents do for a living, and it can teach them work ethics and entrepreneurship, by their parents' example and by participation in the venture. Some businesses incorporate three and four generations who work as a team—nepotism at its best. One home company has titled each child vice-president, much to his and her delight and pride. (See Tax Benefits.)

Provide your own day care for your children and work from home. Add up all the expenses of holding down a job outside the home and see how much you have to earn from a home job to have an equivalent income.

A secretary I know was earning $175 per week. At the top of her listed expenses was child-care cost for her two children ($60); then gasoline and car upkeep came to $30 per week; cost of maintaining her "office wardrobe" averaged $25 per week. She got this far in itemizing job costs and reached a decision to quit her office job as soon as she could realize $100 per week from a home business. She began her home business with a sign on her grocery store bulletin board; phone calls to colleges to list her availability for typing assignments, theses, and dissertations; and an announcement sent to local office managers about her service. Her goal of $100 a week started to come in after the first two weeks. Yes, she worked weekends and nights and held onto her office job. Now, after being in business six months, she sometimes still works long hours, but she is clearing $400 to $500 per week. The investment—a good typewriter being paid off in monthly installments. Now she is shopping for a word processor as part of future plans to increase her earning power.

We all hear about the empty nest syndrome—how women become depressed when the children leave home. A friend of mine who has a homebased public relations firm and is a mother of three grown sons responds to inquiries about her emotional state as son-by-son flew the nest—"I'm elated; I don't lose a son, I gain another office."

MOTHERHOOD

Motherhood has had a serious effect on the careers and aspirations of many women. In the past, a choice had to be made between the satisfaction of having a family *or* having a job. Women began postponing having children, keeping a nervous eye on their biological clock. In the past eight years, the number of expectant mothers in their mid-thirties has almost doubled.

The effect of motherhood on promising careers has been a strain. For some it has slowed down their fast track to the top; others have dropped out; but those who insist on having it all are left with limited time for their children.

Look at the dilemma of the woman who wants to stay home and raise her children but also wants financial independence and a means of self-development. A business at home can satisfy both needs.

When a computer business consultant became a mother, she switched her job arrangement so she could do most of her work from home. She had a computer terminal installed and uses it to communicate with clients on such specialized problems as adopting minicomputers to their operations and writing software programs.

DIVORCED AND ON YOUR OWN

There seems to be a sequence of changing titles—"divorcée" often follows "wife." The fastest growing divorce rate is for couples who have been married for many years. This often leaves the housewife who has no other career no alternative to managing on an inadequate divorce settlement. Spouse support, if any, is often limited to too few years for the woman to return to school, retool, and reenter the job market with more than basic skills.

In my career consultant practice, many of my clients are divorcées lacking professional skills to earn a living. Their panic is real, their anger justifiable. At middle age it is unlikely they can begin at the bottom and catch up with their ex-husband's earning power.

A presiding judge of California Superior Court family law said recently "divorced women are left financially worse off. Lacking good job experience they must accept entry-level jobs paying $900 to $1200 a month before taxes. *Unless they can open a small business that is well capitalized* there just are not that many opportunities out there."

Beginning a business from home can be a very practical move. It can resolve two major dilemmas: the economic problems of the present and the economic potential of the future.

HANDICAPPED

People with a disability who cannot find outside employment or who have to stay home welcome a homebased business. How sad it is for people who could derive satisfaction and income from work to have so few opportunities to do so. One successful homebased baker who happens to be handicapped began making cakes and cookies just to have something to fill time. An overabundance of idle hours led to overproduction and to more sweets than the family could consume. You know what happened next, don't you? Now the deadline for placing Christmas orders for cookies is the first of October! And are they ever good!

The typesetter for my first book was handicapped from a back injury suffered in his football days. His typography service was homebased and much in demand, not because he was handicapped, but because he did excellent work and shared more information about book production than most typographers do.

RETIREES

I hate the word "retirement." I "quit" college teaching, except for occasional seminars (to keep my skills lubricated), because my work life became routine—a signal I experienced in past work that meant leave. If one hangs in there like so many people do, it's not fair to oneself or the consumer.

However, I am not "retired." I am excited once again by new ideas and projects. The difference is I can now keep a more flexible schedule.

My home office is in operation full-time. Working from home provides so many like me with a productive activity in terms of interest, money, continued involvement, and personal growth.

I urge all "retirees" to stay involved in business. Otherwise you may hear this: "I married you for better or worse, but not to cook three meals a day." Unaccustomed twenty-four-hour intimacy can be just as tough on the spouse as it is on the retiree.

Turn a hobby into a business. The only difference between a hobby and a business is one you do for pleasure and the other you do for pleasure and monetary gain. New interests are a blessed addition to conversation; otherwise focused on "What's for dinner?" or "Where is the television program?"

Rustproof Your Retirement*

Retirement doesn't have to be a red light. It can be a green light. Othmar Ammann would agree. After he "retired" at age sixty, he designed, among other things, the Connecticut and New Jersey turnpikes; the Pittsburgh Civic Arena; Dulles Airport; the Throgs Neck Bridge; and the Verrazano Narrows Bridge. Paul Gauguin "retired" as a successful stockbroker and became a world-famous artist. Heinrich Schliemann "retired" from business to look for Homer's legendary city of Troy. He found it. After Churchill made his mark as a world statesman, he picked up his pen and won the Nobel prize for literature at age seventy-nine. Don't just go fishing when you retire. Go hunting. Hunt for the chance to do what you've always wanted to do. Then go do it!

*Reprint Permission from United Technologies

An eminent physician wrote in his syndicated newspaper column that a "beautifully engraved gold watch and a department luncheon hardly compensates for the sense of abandonment that so many people feel because of retirement at an early age—sixty-five years." He endorses returning to the mainstream of activity and to replace the "burden" of leisure with the joys of accomplishment.

An eighty-one-year-old North Dakota artist calls a rest home his home. His hand-tied rag rugs began as occupational therapy but demand by collectors is so great he works a twelve-hour day! Age hasn't slowed up a seventy-year-old chemist, but canker sores and other dental problems did annoy him. Adding aloe, a gel extracted from the aloe vera plants, to a conventional toothpaste formula produced a cure for his problem. He's a one-employee company, driving around the U.S., and selling to more than seven hundred drug and food outlets, persuading buyers that the public would buy an expensive toothpaste, three times the cost of most other brands, and they are.

My typist is eighty-two years old and certainly qualifies for society's idea of retirement age. Not to her, it doesn't! With her home office, a part-time job, college classes, she still finds time to jog around the campus track.

Statistics indicate that work interest is an important factor in longevity. A recent study based on a follow-up of social security recipients determined that the "long-lived" continued to work, whether it be in their gardens or at jobs outside the home. I admire Avanti Motors, whose business practices have included hiring the older worker and I do mean older—employees in the sixty to eighty age bracket. And, in return, Avanti says they produce a better car. I believe it.

INCOME INSURANCE

Our uncertain economy has made people wary about the certainty of their jobs. It is reassuring to have a faithful standby employer—you!

Remember the engineers and their plight in the 1973–75 recession? Engineers and mechanics who had thought themselves immune to job layoffs were stunned to be included in industry's budget trimmings. Eventually many were recalled to their jobs and vowed that they wouldn't wait for the ax to fall again. They decided to try and build their own security by moonlighting as carpenters, upholsterers, salesmen, and welders. They turned backyard sheds into car repair shops and basements into photography studios. Some of these people have returned to school to refine their skills, turning what was once a hobby into a living.

Not only engineers experienced long-term unemployment, but other large groups: schoolteachers, tire producers, auto mechanics, and flight controllers. Have they been able to survive without losing their homes and draining their bank accounts? Are their personal relationships surviving the strain?

Don't let it happen to you!

NEVER TOO OLD

Victim of age discrimination? Never if you are in charge. Joblessness strikes older men and women especially hard. Just when they expect to be rewarded for years of honesty, loyalty, and service to employers, reaching the firing age of fifty-five years leaves older workers vulnerable to the age bias of their bosses. No need to cover up the graying hair, get a face-lift or jog yourself into the orthopedist's office— that's if you hire *yourself* for life. Where can you find employees today with the work values and ethics of the fifty-five-and-older generation?

HEALTH AND HEARTH

People who have worked "out" swear when they switched to working "in" that they saved money on doctor bills. There is less wear and tear on the body and less stress. More creativity emerges. It may take an adjustment period, but soon the homebased person can find some time for gardening, painting, reading, or whatever that is almost impossible to arrange in an outside-job lifestyle except on those rare days off.

SAVINGS

Imagine the homebased person's savings on personal wardrobe and grooming. Ah-h-h, to work in your ancient bathrobe, jeans, or the costume of your choice. Reduced consumption of gasoline, by becoming a one-car family or by not having to use your second car for a daily commute, will show sizable savings.

Eating your own home cooking at your own kitchen counter is another savings, as well as a pleasant change from lunches out or the brown bag. You know what's in your hamburger heaven.

COMPETITION

Cutting down on overhead means that you can charge less than competitors with outside locations. Most customers are quite price-conscious and accustomed to shopping for the best prices for goods and services.

Another kind of competition that homebased business eliminates is the office variety—competing to get recognition from the boss.

ECOLOGICAL ECONOMY

Homebased working offers efficient utilization of space. Why take up twice the amount of space in the world if one place will serve two needs—living and working. Keeping your car at home helps to reduce pollution, reduces fuel consumption, and eases overcrowded freeways, streets, and roads. Not only are homeworkers making a significant contribution to saving the world's energy resources, but they are conserving their own resources.

THE BUSINESS IS THE PROPERTY

If you are able to buy property where you and the business can live, that's a business investment in itself, building equity. Judging by today's appreciated real estate market, tomorrow's may be better yet. Property can be used as collateral, and constitutes a forced savings account.

LESS PAPERWORK—FEWER EMPLOYEES

When your business grows and production requires more hands, an outside contractor can be hired who, in turn, contracts with others to do piecework in their homes. The contractor distributes the raw materials, inspects and pays each home-worker, and returns the finished product to you. Your payroll consists of one person: the contractor.

When more help is needed, it is simpler to use a contractor, rather than hiring employees. There is less bookkeeping expense and fewer records for you to keep.

A public relations "firm" (a boss and a part-time secretary) provide any service requested by the client. How can a staff of one and one-half do all the work? They don't. Graphic artists are hired to take care of brochures and stationery, caterers are hired for dinner parties given for the clients' clients, and other professionals are hired for tasks that relate to image creation and promotion. Don't say "no" to requests when you are building your business.

TAX BENEFITS

Caution: Do consult a homebased accountant when planning and starting your homebased business and before filing your income tax. (See Resources for list of IRS Tax Publications.)

Deductions for business use of your home is one of the

21

great advantages of a homebased business. Usually, you can take a percentage of your normal home-operating costs as business deductions.

The tax savings on home offices can be significant. The footage set aside *exclusively* and *regularly* for work and office can be deducted. Using part of your living room as an office, IRS rules can be satisfied by isolating the space either by the arrangement of the furniture and/or screening off an area. If business items are stored in a garage, attic, or closet, that space can be deducted.

Here's how IRS defines these two words:

Exclusive use of a portion of your home means you must use a specific part of your home *solely* for the purpose of conducting your business or employment. If you use a portion of your home as your business office and also for personal purposes, you have *not* met the exclusive-use requirement.

Regular use means you must use the exclusive business portion of your home on a continuing basis. The occasional or incidental use of a portion of your home doesn't meet the "regular use" requirement even if that portion of your home is used for no other purpose.

Because of much protest, the treasury department has eased its stand on home offices. The IRS recently reversed its stand and issued a rule allowing a deduction for a home office as the main place for a secondary business.

For business usage you must determine the size of your total living space and then the percentage of that total which is devoted to the business. This can be done on the basis of square footage or number of rooms if your rooms are fairly comparably sized. In a five-room apartment where you weave in one room, one-fifth (or 20 percent) of the total is business usage.

DEDUCTIONS.
On that basis, you may figure your deductions as 20 percent of rent, utility bills, household insurance, real estate taxes, mortgage interest (but not principal), repairs, pest control, improvements, any expense that applies to the house as a

whole. Any expenditures totally for the business area, such as a special floor covering, are totally deductible.

If you have customers and clients coming to the house to transact business, you are entitled to deduct the cost of keeping up appearances. Gardening, cleaning services, repairs, and installation of special business equipment, are deductible.

The expense of operating an automobile, a truck, or a van used for business is deductible. If the use of the vehicle is combined for personal convenience also, the amount of driving done for business is prorated. Check with your accountant about car depreciation. If you need your capital for start-up, consider leasing a car.

When something purchased for your business during the fiscal year has a useful life of longer than a year—a briefcase, a home computer, a calculator, a word processor—you will have to decide about how to deduct the expenditure. The expense can be depreciated over a long period, typically five years, or for the first time you can write off the entire cost, up to $5,000, in one year. The Internal Revenue Service (IRS) has many free publications that provide information and guidelines (See Resources.) Get them. Read them. Then discuss with your accountant which is the best way for you to take the depreciation.

If you own or are buying the property, you may figure depreciation of your business portion of the house. If your house costs $30,000 (excluding the land) and you are using one-third of it for your studio, then your depreciation basis is $10,000. Spread over perhaps twenty years, you could deduct $500 per year in depreciation. When you decide to sell your home, there are tax laws that affect the deductions you have been taking for a home office.

Your deduction for an office in the home cannot exceed the gross income generated that year from the business. If this happens, there is a definite order in which deductions can be taken.

TAX-SAVING CHILDREN

The *Professional Report* notes that: ''Since employee salaries and benefits are tax deductible to your business, you can cut down double taxation by employing family members. You'll get a particularly favorable tax break when you hire your minor children. As long as you supply more than half of the child's support and he or she is under age nineteen or goes to school full-time for five months out of the year, you can claim the child as a dependent on your tax return. The child, in turn, can claim a $1,000 personal exemption plus the $2,300 zero bracket amount on his or her return. Thus, if one child works for you, your family will gain $3,000 of nontaxable income.''

TAX-SAVING ''HOBBIES''

Hobbies turned into businesses comprise an ego-satisfying validation of pleasurable work and are tax-saving. When the pastime becomes a full-time business, you can take deductions larger than the income from your ''hobby.'' It can also create a shelter for other income. If you manage to make a profit in any two years within a five-year period, the Internal Revenue Service will assume automatically that your hobby is a business. Even if you cannot pass the two-out-of-five year test, you may well be able to convince the IRS that you are sincerely trying to make a profit. Keep accurate and up-to-date records, showing that you work hard at your avocation. The tax court may let you claim losses unredeemed by profits for a decade or more.

OFF-THE-RECORD ECONOMY

''Off-the-Books Business Booms in Europe'' is a headline from *The Wall Street Journal*. I read the article expecting to learn something about publication. Instead it deals, in part, with what homebased business is about—extra incomes—work performed off the books, receiving cash payment that goes unrecorded. The French call this activity *travail au noir*, the Italians *lavoro nero*, the Germans *schwarza beiter*, and the British, simply, *fiddling*.

''The prevailing British attitude on the matter of fiddling is evident in a recent public-opinion survey. Only 31 percent of Britons polled felt that it was wrong to avoid paying taxes on money earned in your spare time.'' Far higher percentages felt it was wrong to engage in fox hunting (59 percent) or "miss work and tell your employer you were ill when you were not" (62 percent).

This underground activity is estimated to be 35 percent of the aboveground counterpart in Europe. This is a higher percentage than in the U.S., economists say, mainly because of the higher taxes in western Europe. The IRS says self-employed individuals are the least likely to accurately report their income. Figures indicate that only 60 percent of income is reported. Dinner parties become business entertainment; vacations are business trips.

Under-the-table money is what Americans call it. It may be a big temptation, but covering your tracks is more trouble than it is worth. My feelings about this matter? I don't mind one bit paying *all* taxes due for the space I take up in our *free* society.

Smoke Gets in Your Eyes

> *O money, money, money I'm not nec-*
> *essarily one of those who think thee holy,*
> *But I often stop to wonder how thou canst*
> *go out so fast when thou comest in so*
> *slowly.*
>
> —Ogden Nash

There could possibly be a counterargument for each of the listed advantages of home-work, but the major disadvantages are you can't call in sick! Every day is Monday! and the harder you work the ''luckier'' you'll be!

SELF-MOTIVATION

Without an imposed work structure, you have to get yourself up in the morning. No competitive coworkers, no boss. ''Just one more cup of coffee'' is tempting and giving in to nonwork moods too often is self-defeating. It may result in missed deadlines, reduced quotas, and a diminished sense of pride and confidence.

Tying up the business phone for personal chats makes for an uneasy sense of undeserved pleasure. You could be calling clients or working on public relations and promotion of your product or service.

Can you count on self-motivation? And how will you feel when your drive and determination take a vacation?

EGO SHOCK

"When I was an executive at the bank, I had no problem getting an appointment with anyone. Now that I am in my own management business, I can call over a hundred prospective clients and not get a single appointment. Sometimes I feel totally frustrated and ineffective."

How do you take rejection? Anticipate that sometimes you will think your business is a cemetery; will you be able to raise your own spirits in spite of all the well-wishers' caveat: "I told you not to leave that good job."

HARD, HARD WORK

It isn't luck that's going to make your business a success. Count on seventy to eighty hours a week. Forget eight hours sleep a night—perhaps a half day off on Sundays—forget tennis, forget your hobbies.

A National Federation of Independent Business study states that more than half of all small-business owners work at least sixty hours in the start-up year, and 25 percent work more than seventy hours.

ADVICE ADDICTION

At a homebased business seminar in San Francisco, I recognized a couple of people from the year before. "How come you are back again?" I asked. "We wanted to hear your 'advice' again."

It's a good thing to do: tap people, such as experts or business owners who are established or "retired" to go to for advice. Even suppliers can be a good resource. "Be prepared" is a worthy credo.

But advice has its limits. Some people can never get enough advice before taking off—and then more than likely they will never take off. Just like the woman who approached me during a break in a seminar to tell me she had the best idea for a business these past twenty years.

THE GAMBLE

Who wants to have to feel optimistic all the time? How do you handle failure—your own, that is? Have you ever had to fire yourself? If you don't succeed, will you try and try again? It's a risky ego trip to be an entrepreneur. Can you afford the dry spells when there's no business?

INTERRUPTIONS

Can you cope with your three-year-old tugging at your ~nees, and joyful dogs wanting you to play fetch, while you ~e negotiating a business deal on the phone? Family and friends drop in because they "know you are home." A dress designer complains that her neighbors do not take her work seriously because it is homebased. They always send their children over to play at her house. No matter how considerate you try to be, it is likely that being firm about social infringements on your work time will offend some people.

TOGETHERNESS

If the rest of your family also is homebased, togetherness, on a twenty-four-hour basis sometimes becomes suffocating. You may yearn for an opportunity to be alone. Trust yourself in relation to this need and treat it seriously. There are ways to arrange some solitude for yourself if you are determined to do so. You may be pleasantly surprised at your family's response to "I love you all dearly, but right now I need to be alone and undisturbed."

ISOLATION

The homebased business can result in virtual isolation, removing you from the mainstream, and some people react to this problem by becoming reclusive and even agoraphobic. Most of us have some need of a work group, colleagues for companionship, exchange of ideas, and competitive spirit in order to produce our best work.

Professional organizations and business clubs of various

kinds can be a boon to the lone, homebased worker. One home-worker I know makes certain she has social engagements several evenings each week, just to be sure there is a balance in her life.

SECURITY

Initial financial sacrifices and no more steady paychecks require an adjustment. How much will you miss the fringe benefits, company-paid health plans, paid vacations (or just vacations), and pension plans? After a client, a custom stationer, left a paper company to begin his own business, his earnings the first week were one dollar forty-seven cents. Can you cope with that possibility?

BUSINESS CLAUSTROPHOBIA

Our house, until the business moved in, had four bedrooms. To date, the businesses have spread like uncontrollable lava through three bedrooms, the four-car garage, and at times we sense a warm, molten flow around our feet! It is difficult to confine a home business to its designated place, but failure to do so can be irritating to spouse or other family members. They may feel "edged out" of their own home.

NETWORKING

It is essential to let people know about you, to go to professional and business organization meetings and to speaking engagements. Talking about yourself and what you do at every opportunity makes you hunger for anonymity and a chance to talk about the weather, but it will promote your business.

JILL- OR JACK-OF-ALL-TRADES

It may be okay for Jack or Jill—but is it okay for you? Can you be the producer, bookkeeper, salesperson, secretary, promoter, shipper . . . ? Business stops when you do!

BYE-BYE, DREAM

There's the risk of success. Ironically, if it becomes too big, your business may throw you out of your house. What happens then to the pleasures of working from home?

NO RELIEF IN SIGHT

There's that "never finished" feeling. Remember the occasions you had to take work home from the office to complete it? Well, you *are* home! There's *always* unfinished business. There's no distance between you and it. Its accessibility may be too close for comfort.

Homebased working presents an almost irresistible temptation to the incipient workaholic. The workshop, the desk, the work are always close at hand.

IMPOSED HOSPITALITY

There's the invasion-of-privacy factor. How do you feel about strangers sitting on *your* toilet seat? Clients coming to a home setting expect to be wined and dined, to use your bathroom, to look into your medicine chest, and to make you put your dog, cat, and child out of the room because of their allergies. How do you deal with a customer's "Do you mind if I smoke?" if it's against house rules, or "May I use your phone?" when the phone bill is already too high?

RESENTMENT

Imagine a situation with both husband and wife working but one of them is dashing off to work at an outside employment and the other, home-employed, is still in a terry robe, enjoying the morning newspapers. This scene has brought down many a marital curtain. One partner envies the other's automatic company paycheck, while the second partner wishes for the "easy" lifestyle.

How do you divide the chores? "Dishes, anyone?" The homebased person may have to become more assertive to achieve an equitable division of household responsibilities and chores.

HOMEBASED CALORIES

The refrigerator is too hospitable to us hard (home) workers. If you have difficulty controlling your weight, keep only enough food around for survival. Eating a gallon of rocky road ice cream to celebrate, to drown sorrows, and/or to stall returning to work could become a disastrous habit.

APPEARANCE

And there's the temptation to never get out of your "sweats"—"they are so comfortable" and "isn't this one of the reasons working at home is so attractive—not to have to get dressed up?" Of course, you are right on all counts. Just because you *are* homebased it's important to look professional. So-o-o when a client is coming to your door that Rip Van Wrinkly look has to go, hair groomed, no dust under your fingernails, and the house straightened, and aired.

The client can look a mess but you are the one who has to build customer confidence and how you look does make a difference. Keep in mind as you are "dressing up" for the appointment you can start stripping down as soon as the car drives off.

> *The great advantage of a hotel is that it's*
> *a refuge from a homebased business.*
> —BNF

Now that you know almost all the pros and cons of a homebased business, let's get down to the nitty-gritty of becoming an entrepreneur and the boss—and the company's only employee.

The Eight P's of Planning A Business

Business is other people's money.
—Delphine de Girardin

Here are major considerations for small businesses as well as for big businesses—both need to take the same steps, using the same formula before opening their doors.

- PRODUCTS and/or SERVICES
  What kind of business do I want?
- PEOPLE
  Who and how many customers do I estimate will use my services or buy my products?
- PLACE
  Is the proposed space in my home adaptable to my business?
- PRICE
  What should I charge?
- PROTECTION
  Do I need insurance, copyright, or patent?
- PROMOTION
  What will be the methods of marketing and advertising?
- PERSISTENCE
  Do I have what it takes—the drive to work hard with optimism?
- PROBLEMS of SUCCESS
  Have I anticipated the new challenges that any start-up business faces when the public says yes, Yes, YES!

HOW WELL-SUITED RICK BECAME WELL-HEELED—
AN EXAMPLE OF THE EIGHT PRINCIPLES

Rick built a million-dollar-a-year retail menswear business by selling discount clothing out of an apartment in a suburban neighborhood. His business thrives on professionals who are willing to spend a lot of money on clothes "that make the man." About five years ago, when Rick first decided to sell clothes out of his apartment, he had only enough stock to fill one closet. Now that apartment is lined with clothing racks and shelves. Customers try on clothing in Rick's bathroom. The business has grown so rapidly that Rick soon began hiring salespeople and now employs twelve part-time salespeople. Rick's business is a good example of how a homebased business is born and of how skills used for someone else's business (he had been a salesperson in a retail clothing store) can be used for one's own business.

First, Rick knew his goal—to make a lot of money. He also recognized his skills and assets: a knack for selling, friendliness, and persistence. Rick had experience, too. Since the age of fifteen, he had been selling fine men's clothes and had the experience of designing and marketing men's cuff links. While still in high school, Rick bought after-sale topline men's clothes from retail stores and resold them to his friends and acquaintances and at swap meets.

How Rick used the P's of planning to establish his business:

STEP 1—PRODUCT.
Fine menswear; discount operation.

STEP 2—PEOPLE.
Rick had tested (in his fashion) to see if there was a market for this product and decided that there was. As a salesman in a retail store, he discovered that (a) men really do not like to go shopping for their wardrobes; but (b) they will spend money if they feel that they are being outfitted properly; and (c) a customer's confidence in his own taste grows as he puts together complete outfits with coded labels to help him remember what to wear with what; and (d) the clientele Rick sought was quality-conscious and label-conscious.

STEP 3—PLACE.

Rick started selling from his apartment because he could not afford a storefront. He got a business license; however, his landlord did not like Rick's conducting business from the building, so Rick had to move to another apartment where the owner did not mind. A person with less perseverance might have been deterred completely by the first landlord.

STEP 4—PRICE.

No consumers would go out of their way to buy clothes at regular prices. But they will go out of their way for a bargain. Manufacturers get stuck with overstock and will sell to discounters despite the pressure from retailers not to sell to discounters. One way to convince manufacturers to sell to a discounter is to offer to change the labels in the clothes. Rick uses an Yves St. Germain label. He also sells accessories to go with the clothes, which helps to build up his sales and his profits.

Buying designer clothes at discount was very appealing to Rick's clientele. The bathroom dressing room seemed to make no difference to his customers—perhaps it reinforced the bargain aspect of his operations.

STEP 5—PROTECTION.

Insurance for theft, damage, and liability.

STEP 6—PROMOTION.

In addition to the word-of-mouth advertising he depended on, Rick hired an advertising agency to enable him to reach a larger market. They drew up an ad that read ''Would You Change in My Bathroom to Save $200?'' It ran monthly in a popular Los Angeles magazine with a large circulation directed toward young, on-the-way-up people. Its subscribers are middle- and upper-middle class.

Because of the unique operation and through customer contacts, Rick appeared on many television and radio interviews. This sort of thing helps advertise a product. Just think what the time would cost if it was bought on prime-time television. He got a free plug (credit) daily on a TV show because he provided the clothes for the male talk show host. Rick also uses mailers to advertise.

STEP 7—PERSISTENCE.

Go back to Step 4. Though he was evicted from his first "store" apartment, Rick was determined to give his business concept a try and found an amiable landlord. Another payoff of his persistence was convincing manufacturers to sell to him.

STEP 8—PROBLEMS OF SUCCESS.

His present concerns are avoiding what he calls the problems of successful entrepreneurs, such as trying to do too much of the work himself and expanding too rapidly. When he began the homebased operation, he was in his twenties. Because of customer demand, he now has a large men's clothing store with a celebrity clientele.

Products or Services? Finding a Business

> *Creation comes before distribution—or there will be nothing to distribute.*
> —Ayn Rand

Let's get started by assuming that you do not have the slightest idea for a homebased business. There are several approaches to finding what it is you can and want to do. The ultimate occupation is one that you love doing and earns money. But, alas, the majority of the work force work for the paycheck and are either bored, blue, or burned-out with their work. My goal is to help people "work happy."

How to Find a Business

- **Transfer nine-to-five skills home.**
- **Turning a hobby into a paying business.**
- **Learning new skills or improving present ones.**
- **Marketing a new service or product.**
- **Improving an existing product or service.**
- **Utilizing hidden assets.**
- **Doing your homework.**

What you can do:

Transfer the skills presently used at a nine-to-five job to a home base. Secretarial skill is a natural for this and many typists all over the country are now offering secretarial services from home. The numbers are large enough to have formed a national organization with local chapters, publish their own newsletter, and hold a national conference yearly. Some have diversified to include additional services such as typography, résumé-writing, graphic design, telephone an-

36

swering service, become notaries, and even provide temporary office help. One self-transferred home typist wrote and self-published a book—you guessed right—it's on how to become an independent at-home typist.

A pharmacologist who knew the difficulty that independent drug stores, clinics, and hospitals experience in finding relief pharmacists began an employment agency for temporary and permanent positions as a moonlighting business. He works a four-to-midnight shift at a drugstore.

After twelve years with one of the largest international accounting firms a CPA-lawyer I know converted one of the rooms in his home to an office and now has a very successful practice there. He says instead of putting in a concentrated ten-hour day for an employer, depriving both himself and his children of family life, he can now interrupt his home-work to take the kids to Little League practice. No longer an absentee papa who only pays for rather than plays with his kids.

A car mechanic blew a gasket when his employer, an automobile agency, informed him that commission split would be 60/40 and, of course, you know who was to get the 60 percent. He's now a traveling car-doctor, makes house calls just like the plumber.

Can a hobby be turned into a money-making business?
Snugli Inc. had sales in the millions. Not bad for an outfit that started as a hobby. A Snugli is a pouchlike device made of cloth in which people carry infants. The designer had noticed while on a stint with her husband in the Peace Corps how African babies were carried close to the mother's body. She fashioned a device so that she, too, could carry her first child African-style. Much of the sewing for this product is still done by women in their homes.

Many craft and folk artists began their work just for their own pleasure but when admirers became purchasers . . . well, it became a business. The market is particularly ripe now for artisans. People are making a ''hobby'' of collecting, so artists have purposely coaxed their craft into producing an income.

Are you the friendly, kind neighbors' fix-it person? The person they call when the electric socket shorts out, the garbage in the disposal comes up rather than down and they are so appreciative when their life's back in order that for payment they thank you and thank you and offer you a cup of coffee. Okay, Fix-it Person, hang out your shingle (zoning permitting), pass out your calling cards, and it's cash-on-the-line.

There's satisfaction in getting paid for doing something you have done before but was solely for your own pleasure. That's what hobbies are all about. It doesn't have to develop into one of those million-dollar businesses unless that's your goal. If what you want is to just feel productive and make a few extra bucks a week, hobbies are hidden dividends.

Are you willing to learn or improve a skill through attending classes, apprenticeship, or teaching yourself? Laura Ashley, the fabric design mogul, did. She taught herself fabric printing from a library book and now sixteen factories later has 113 retail shops worldwide.

Have you an idea for a new service or a product? Some of the best seem to have been overlooked by market pros. Look what has happened to the computer explosion: manufacturers, programmers, service force, how-to books, consultants and teachers, even a language all its own. Admittedly, that example is a biggie. But could you have anticipated the exotic fruit and flower boom in the United States? Or such services as exercisers, plant tenders, image consultants, diet nutritionists, animal psychologists filling needs and meeting with such success?

Do you have an idea to improve, market, or promote a product or service that is already on the market? ''I didn't invent the hamburger. I just took it more seriously than anyone else,'' says the founder of McDonald's.

Many people think that unless you come up with a real new product you won't come up with anything big. Many big winners, in fact, are products that anyone could have invented by using readily available parts, ingredients, or technology. Razors and lighters were on the market but someone thought up the idea of making them disposable. And what about umbrellas . . . who was the genius who thought of bending one to fit into a briefcase?

A forty million-dollar winner is a special kind of notepaper. The same old notepad that we all have used, except this kind has stickum on the back so it can be stuck on telephones, walls, bulletin boards, and desks, displacing the thumbtack. This idea came to a member of a church choir whose slips of paper used to mark songs in a hymnbook kept falling out. Someone else had presented a similar idea to the manufacturer ten years before and was turned down.

There are old markets where a small gap may exist and you can capitalize on it. An example is the success of a tie salesman who decided to go into his own homebased tie business after seventeen years experience working for someone else. With so many well-established tie manufacturers why does he have so little competition with his ties. . . . because he designs ties with custom logos tastefully woven into the fabrics. Corporations order ties with their emblems for their executives, sales force, and their customers. He also designs for the tastes and whims of all those female customers who buy his "V.I.P." (very important person) and other "message" designs such as "Hello Handsome." His four-year-old business had sales of $1 million last year and what is remarkable is that he is the head designer, bookkeeper, salesman, order-taker, typist, shipping clerk, and telephone operator. He doesn't want his neckwear business to get too big.

"I'm not," he says, "looking to grow so much I have to move out of the house."

Do you have hidden assets in your home? List the rooms in your home, a garage, a barn, and yard, if you have one. Can tourism be taken advantage of by the geographical location? Vacationers looking for something different find farms, ranches, and rural lodges from Oregon to New England offer an ideal solution. Want to share the good life with city dwellers? For those of you who are city dwellers and want to make your dwelling help with the overhead, see the section on The Home as a Product. Some of the suggestions are Bed and Breakfast, Living Room Classes, Yard/Garage/Barn Sales, Foster Care, Hideaways. . . . What businesses can the rooms generate?

Living rooms provide the setting for classrooms, exercise studios, selling of products, the Home Party business, galleries, fortune-tellers. Even bathrooms lead a double life as dressing rooms, hair salons. One newsletter publisher employs five who show up daily to his New York apartment and the toilet seat has a typewriter sitting on it. Two balloonery companies that I am familiar with began their business in the bathroom, storing the helium tanks in the bathtub.

Yard sales are held in front of apartment buildings and houses, not just on a Saturday or Sunday but daily. Some specialize, such as bric-a-brac or furniture. There's a frame house in east Los Angeles that always has two or three used refrigerators with For Sale signs leaning against the porch railing. And owners will take monthly payments. Home furnishings can be put to work to bring in income. Consider them material assets. List the things you own: stove, refrigerator, iron, sewing machine, car, telephone, tape recorder, TV, and all the rest of those products we have been sold. Now they can earn their own keep and make their own payments.

Here's how some entrepreneurs have converted their **hidden assets** into businesses:

Telephone.
>   Sales, your company or someone else's.
>   Answering Service/Message Center.
>   Dial-for-Justice—Clients pay to have someone else fight their bureaucratic battles.
>   Children's Story Hour—For a monthly fee the child can dial and listen to a short nighty-night story.
>   U.S. Inns Telephone Directory—for subscribers.
>   Astrological Forecast—for subscribers.
>   Dial-a-Soap—for subscribers who miss their favorite programs and want to know what happened.

Mailbox.
>   Mail order.

Car.
>   Taxi or rent by the day to another driver.
>   Driving Instruction.
>   Teach Auto Repair.
>   Messenger Service.
>   Pick-up and deliver people to their place of work for a monthly fee, or home delivery for stores, messenger service.

Washing Machine/Dryer.
>See Washerwoman under Services.

Stove.
>Working people pick up a home-cooked meal from another cook's kitchen. Fresh breads, pastries, candies, jams. One chef calls his business "The Soup Kitchen" because a choice of soups is all he provides.

Get the idea? For other suggestions check the lists under Products and Services. People all over the country are putting their personal assets to work. You can, too.

Doing your homework is true research.

The inspiration for a business can be sparked by an article in a newspaper, magazine, OR THIS BOOK! Make it a practice to go to the newsstands or library when the monthly magazines hit the stands. Check the table of contents of the appropriate periodicals for an article of interest. Become a browser. Clip, file, and save any information about any of the eight P's of planning a business. Even articles that are targeted for big business have some lessons that are applicable to your business.

In this book there are lists of examples of homebased businesses in current operation in the U.S. One of them just might be right for you and right for your community or right for the rest of us.

Consider yourself lucky if you can choose the kind of work that makes you happy AND get paid for it. Statistics affirm about forty years of one's life is spent working and it's up to you to determine the quality of that work life. Shakespeare in *The Merchant of Venice* writes "He is well paid that's well satisfied."

People: Potential Customers

*My interest is in the future because I am
going to spend the rest of my life there.*
—Charles F. Kettering

**Is there a need for your product or service?
Who are your potential customers?
How can you get this information?**

The fact is that few entrepreneurs actually do a great deal
of market research. They are so eager to get started, they
are just not willing to do all the homework. I know from
the reaction of many clients when I give them a list of
research-related tasks to do.

New businesses seldom can afford professional market research. But you can make an informed estimate about the
potential of your business venture. Homebased businesses
can be approached with some of the same considerations
given to any other enterprise. Procter and Gamble and General Foods always obtain a sampling of consumer reaction
to new products prior to nationwide distribution.

Big business relies on such techniques as phone surveys,
mailed questionnaires, or extensive test-marketing, facts
culled from published materials such as surveys and census
data. An exploding homebased business is a computerized
data base operation that supplies compiled information on
any market research assignment for clients.

The cost of "bought" market research is usually more
than the entrepreneur had planned to invest in the whole
business! As one market expert put it "the cost of making
something happen is less than the cost of measuring whether
it can happen."

Typical of the kind of research small-time operators do is
that based on personal inventory. What they like they think
others will, too; what they need they think others do, too.

And many times they are accurate. Six years ago, a female runner began her running-wear business, knowing nothing about designing or sewing clothes, but knowing from her own experience that her running shorts fit poorly. Like just about every other pair on the market they were cut for the male physique, causing too tight a fit on a woman's rear. That was the extent of her research. Her company has a small niche in that specialized business, in 1982 about $3 million compared to an estimated $130 million for the entire running-wear industry.

Would you believe that a husband-wife team got into a very successful business because they love goats! Professional market researchers would definitely frown on how they developed their product. Kinda like the cart before the horse, or in this case, the goat. First they bought goats, then what to do with all that goat milk, and to resolve that problem—goat cheese. He, weary of academic life, thought they might make a go of it, believing a market existed for the delicacy. Could they have foreseen that goat cheese has replaced Brie cheese in demand and that the better food retailers prefer buying from quality small producers such as they are. Success.

Two clients, partners, came to me—*after the fact*—to ask why their mail-order item had not sold. They had placed expensive ads several times in the magazine sections of *The New York Times* and the *Los Angeles Times*.

What was the item? Pajama bottoms for men. They had so convinced themselves that it was a great, original idea that they had gone ahead and manufactured one thousand pajama bottoms.

When I asked what advance research had been done to indicate or validate their opinion that the public's taste had turned to "bottoms only" in nightwear, their response was . . . "none" . . . other than they "knew" many men sleep in their underwear . . . and since the uppers and lowers of pajamas were not sold separately . . . they "felt" orders would flow in.

What are some of the preliminary market research efforts they should have tried before manufacturing pajama bottoms? Samples could have been shown to buyers of men's clothing for their reaction and samples left at stores to test consumer reaction. Also, questioning nightwear manufacturers as to why *they* make nightshirts and pajamas and *not* pajama separates might have been informative.

Anyone need one thousand P.J. bottoms? Contact me and I'll put you in touch with my clients.

A granola bar caper—eighty thousand ordered by the determined food inventor from a food manufacturing company. He refused to heed their advice to market-test first, convinced the public would love the healthy bar. They might have but the food chain stores did not think they needed to sacrifice shelfspace for *another* granola bar.

Opening a homebased business is a big step for many small-time operators. So let's take care.

- Begin by asking potential customers if they or people they know need this service or would buy this product?
- Place a test ad and see if there are any nibbles. It's really difficult to judge by the initial response, because advertising usually pays off after a period of time. Does the advertising medium selected reach the right audience?
- Size up the competition. How many businesses are offering the same product or service in the small area? If the product is to go national, such as a mail order item, check out all magazines and catalogs to be sure yours is a fresh product.
- Ask the competition how they are doing. Remember they may not encourage your entry into their marketplace because you may be unwanted competition.
- Get advice from consultants in the same field. It is part of information-gathering. They can give important tips and offer shortcut ideas.
- Check the quality and price structure of existing competition. How does your product or service compare?
- Do you have any advantages over the competition? If you do, remember to use this in your promotion and advertising. Will you give more value for the dollar, better service, superior quality, uniqueness? If you are offering a professional service, what advantages do you have over others—more education or experience, or both? This is no time for modesty.
- What disadvantages will you be facing? Don't be afraid to look at the drawbacks. Forewarned is forearmed.
- Gathering information, both pro and con, is a major step for decision-making.

Place

There's no place like Home, Sweet Home.
                              —Anonymous

BUT IS IT LEGAL?

Is it legal to have a business in a home? Everyone asks that! It depends on your city's code, the zoning restrictions, and what you call home. Homebased businesses are housed in apartments, houses, commercial buildings, stores, mobile homes, down in cellars, up in lofts, boats, garages, farmhouses, barns, trailers, vans, warehouses, on front lawns, around the back, in closets, and adjacent buildings.

"It's not fancy, but you can't beat the rent," says North Carolina's legendary on-the-road lawyer about his office. It's a battered 1969 bus equipped with an old typewriter, sleeping bag, kerosene heater, and law books. A parking meter for a landlord?

A meter or a patient's driveway is the underpinning of the small but growing number of mobile services nationwide. For example, dentists have taken to outfitting a motor home with everything necessary to provide care for geriatric patients in retirement complexes, nursing homes, and in rural districts.

Vans are converted to exercise studios, fruit and vegetable markets, food vending, fix-it shops, beauty salons, and barber mobiles—these are some I've seen.

RESIDENTIAL ZONING

More homebased businesses are conducted in residential than in commercial zones. Residential neighborhoods have stricter policies than others. Call the zoning department at your city hall for information, if only to become knowledgeable about the rules and to learn how to bend them through variances and conditional usage permits. Most city zoning departments are too understaffed to enforce the regulations, and emerge only when a complaint has been filed.

COMMERCIAL ZONING

Living behind a store saves money. When Charles Jourdan (International Jourdan Shoe Boutiques) is in Los Angeles, he beds down in a converted small apartment in the back of the store.

"Henry's" has a retail showroom on the first floor of a small commercial building, and a wholesale display section and small, draped-off living quarters on the second floor.

Homebased businesses are under, in front of, behind, and on top of buildings. Lofts in unused downtown warehouses and manufacturing plants have become quite popular for artists who need lots of cheap space. Remember the settings in the film *An Unmarried Woman*? Hundreds of established and not so established artists and gallery operators are fashionably squirreled away in downtown studio lofts, not zoned for domestic occupancy, creating a nouveau Bohemia. They are forming coops, buying up the buildings, because it's practical and preferable to uptown's high rents.

New York's SoHo district and Los Angeles recently made basic changes in the zoning laws allowing artists to obtain a conditional-use permit from the zoning administrator for occupancy in commercial and manufacturing zones. Even the permit fees have been substantially reduced. The structures will still have to meet "eased" existing standards for building and fire requirements. The cities have much to gain: recycling unused, deteriorating vacant buildings, strengthening the economy, creating additional housing, and developing a boon for the contemporary art scene.

If loft living becomes illegal, the artists feel it may be their undoing because if the landlord is still forced to bring the building up to code, the $200 rents will go up and only the wealthier tenants will remain.

Invitations are coveted to the annual Christmas party in the studio-gallery-loft-home of two artists. The hired parking attendants whisk your car away and after you have stepped over the neighborhood assembly of snoring winos, an ancient open elevator laboriously ascends to the loft level, and a butler announces your presence to the other guests.

All the party staff are provided by a friend of the host, who has a homebased business called "Hired Help," specializing in butlers, housekeepers, chauffeurs, governesses, chambermaids, nannies, chefs, valets, and personal maids for the upper crust. This memorable party consumes the artists' yearly advertising budget to promote sales for their paintings. Their sales justify the expense. Each year their work goes up in price and so does the number of buyers.

A famous caricaturist bought a derelict speakeasy on the Upper East Side in New York many years ago. His workroom is on the fourth floor of the converted dwelling. The once run-down neighborhood was discovered by other celebrities and now is fashionable and expensive.

COMPLAINTS AND COMPLIMENTS

If you continue to be the good neighbor you were before your business moved in, it is unlikely that you will have problems with the neighbors. They will complain if your activities create parking problems, are too noisy, or if bad-smelling substances are used in production of a product, if your property becomes unsightly, or if signs advertising the business in a residential neighborhood are hung in the windows.

There's the case of the "sweet smell of vanilla." Neighbors became curious about the delicious baking odors that wafted up the street every day. What had started as Christmas presents for friends, cookies made from a special regional recipe, had grown into a thriving homebased business. Friends wanted to buy them for their friends. That is the way many specialized bakeries begin.

The problem that arose in this operation was the *goodwill* of the neighborhood. People began to drop by regularly to taste what was cooking. The numerous friendly interruptions forced a successful home-baking business out, and into a store.

THE LOCATION

Rent or mortgage payments, apartment or house, make no difference as long as you and yours are ready to give up space for business quarters. It is important to discuss the venture and its needs with other family members to enlist their help and support. Home businesses have a tendency to spread out all over the place; especially vulnerable are kitchen tables, an inviting surface for shipping, bookkeeping, and another cup of tea.

- Is the proposed place for the business appropriate and adaptable? _____ Yes _____ No
- Is location an important factor to the nature of your business? _____ Yes _____ No

If visibility is important, consider an older community where houses and apartments are interspersed with stores. The first floor or the front room of the house can become your showcase. No problems about putting a sign up here.

If the business is conducted by mail and a prestigious address may swell the sales, then rent a post office box from a privately operated postal service. Many of these choose their locations with regard to the frame or popularity or prestige attached to certain streets and areas. An example of this is a post office box with a Wilshire Boulevard, Beverly Hills, address.

These private postal services often offer phone services, too. This sort of service can be workable solutions if your business needs a home away from home, an address in disguise.

CREATING AN OFFICE PLACE

Where is office status rated by how relaxed the living-library feeling prevails? *The Wall Street Journal* reported that *the* executive suites of really powerful corporate bosses look just like home-sweet-home; nary a pen or pencil in sight, and no desk at all. It's a dead giveaway that the corporate occupant lacks status if there's no Oriental rug, no fine paintings on the walls, no adjoining executive dining room, although it's not too "shabby" to have a small dining table and chairs set with Bavarian china by your own butler and cook in the same room as the office. Of course, a wood-burning fireplace. Do any of these features seem familiar? You've already got that homey feeling.

But we do need paper, pen, and pencils and a top of something to work on. Many start on a kitchen table but soon find that's an intrusion. A place for an office is recommended; it lends structure, organization, and privacy. Where space is quite limited a part of a room or a closet will do. There's a newly proposed IRS ruling that a home office does not have to be set apart by a permanent partition. Whether a spare room is utilized, an attic, the garage, or closet, don't shortchange the business by some of the necessary equipment: Storage for stationery, file cabinets, answering machine, typewriter, desktops, bookshelves, storage cabinets, and even looking for paper clips, scissors, staple gun wastes time and energy and holds up progress.

Homebasers who have enough money to equip an office may spend too much time getting set-up just right and avoid growing the business.

Homebasers without money for some office equipment may think they have to wait until they can afford everything to get started. Many of us have used grocery boxes for files, a door on sawhorses for a worktable, those sturdy portable cardboard boxes for storage . . . No excuses, please.

LICENSES AND PERMITS

Remember that many professions require licenses in order to engage in businesses or occupations. Check into the regulations of your state, city, and/or county. Many homebased businesses do not bother to obtain a business license from the city, although the fee is minimal. I prefer keeping legal.

A Board of Health permit may be necessary depending on what and where the cooking's done. Some states restrict selling of products from a home kitchen. Bakers, cooks, candy makers, caterers, and jelly and jam-ers begin and many times remain at home stoves. Home kitchens usually are cleaner than many a restaurant's.

What to do if the demand for your marvelous products outgrows your kitchen? Before you invest in an expensive commercial location and equipment, be cautious, try to rent the off-hours of a restaurant or bakery or ask your temple or church if you can use their kitchen. If their boards refuse because accepting rent might make them lose their nonprofit status, then try bartering . . . agree to an exchange of your products and services for their affairs for use of their commercial kitchen, equal to the rent they would have accepted. Many caterers cook in the client's home to get around the problem of a permit and for convenience. Home garages have been converted to food factories.

Price

My name is Fink
and what do you think?
I press your suit for nothing!
or
I press your suit for nothing?

Depending on the voice inflection, the last line above takes on different meanings. How do you go about setting a *price* for your service or product? Pricing has stymied many a person setting out in business.

FACTORS TO CONSIDER.

If there is any generality to be said about *price*, it is that freelancers, such as photographers, writers, editors, artists, or seamstresses, commonly price themselves *too low* at the outset. It is understandable. In their eagerness to get started their estimation of what the public will pay for their services and/or their products is under market value. You may deliberately underprice to attract a following but the point is to *know* that is what you are doing and to avoid becoming busy with too much work but too little profit. Many businesses have "leader" items, at cost, to bring in the trade, but they make their profit on the rest of the items customers purchase. (It is a common tactic in mail order to develop a mailing list.) But if that is your *only* item, how can you afford to give it away?

It is just as dangerous to set your fee too high. Customers like homebased businesses because the prices are generally lower than store prices. When there is a wide gap between your price and your competition, either too low or too high, people become wary. Only when your homebased business is your second (or third or fourth) job, can you afford to be

51

cavalier about pricing. When the business is your *primary* income, be cautious, giving *pricing* much analysis.

To set a price for a service or product consider these factors:

- **Geography**. There are many factors to be considered in establishing a fee for a service or a price for a product. One of the most significant influences on the amount charged is *geography*. Professional services generally are higher in large cosmopolitan cities than in small cities. Different areas of the country command varying monetary returns for similar services. Think of the cost of housing in Los Angeles compared to Newark. The cost of living varies in different cities—so do services and some products.
- **Numbers**. Some professions practiced in the big cities had to reduce their fees because of the *glut* of their profession in that particular area. Doctors, lawyers, dentists, and psychologists have cloned too many of themselves for the more popular parts of the United States. They have a choice: to stay and try to compete, accepting a slow growth, or move to a less popular community where the competition is no significant threat.
- **Availability**. Another factor in pricing is the *uniqueness* of the product or the service. If you have no competition and there is a consumer demand, charge whatever the market will bear. Products are bought on the basis of their perceived value, not true costs.
- **Comparison**. If you are perplexed about how to find out what to charge, get comparables. Call your competition, as a prospective client or customer, of course, and find out what they are charging. Organizations representing specializations usually have current salary ranges. They can be of help. Comparing prices will help you to arrive at your own.
- **Fame**. If you have achieved *celebrity status* within your field or are working toward that end, charge more as you accumulate the credits. Some of the more renowned have a sliding scale, charging their regular fee to those who can afford their services but less or nothing to those who cannot. I always keep in mind what my veterinarian once advised me—*Never give away a puppy. Charge something because people do not value what they get for free.*

- **Extra Service**. Homebasers build their business reputation on *extra service*. Charges may be the same amount as their outbased competitors but customers know that, if necessary, the at-home typist will work after five. Word-of-mouth advertising gets started not only from customers pleased with the services or products but, in addition, enthusiastic.

  Anyone who works for a living as an artist, and I use that word in its broadest sense, usually has more difficulty in getting a fair return for the time and effort invested. Labors of love sell for too little until the artist is "discovered." It does help that the public appreciates art more today and does more investment buying.

- **Overhead**. Homebased business owners have a tendency to disregard overhead in arriving at a price. Even if you are working on an antique typewriter (I hope you are because of its value today) in the kitchen, *you have expenses*. If you have forgotten what they are, look them up again under Tax Benefits. Remember? The expenses of telephone, gas, and electric bills, rent or mortgage payments, transportation, postage, and so on eat into profits and have to be considered in arriving at a price. Don't guess at the amount of expenses. List them. Successful merchants always know how much it costs them to open the door for business each morning. Although you use your front door for other activities than your business, do not overlook or underplay the significance of operating costs.

- **Time**. There are other kinds of considerations to include in determining price. *Your time is money.* Keep track of your time and do not give it away. If travel is involved to complete an assignment, add up the time and the cost of getting there.

  I have always valued time. It is not a change of attitude because I am passing through middle age. I have never been in the habit of "killing time." Time is my product.

  As your reputation and self-confidence grow, you can increase your fees. You may be forced to whether you want to or not—if the costs of materials and utilities continue to go up. With today's economy, can you think of anything that has a fixed price?

PRODUCT PRICING

Product Pricing. Here is a simple formula to arrive at a price figure for manufacturing a product. There are three main kinds of costs: materials, direct labor, and manufacturing overhead.

MATERIAL	= all materials needed to make the product
LABOR	= cost of workers* who produce product; wages and benefits
MANUFACTURING OVERHEAD	= insurance, utilities, rent, advertising
PRICE	= total costs of materials, labor, manufacturing overhead plus markup.

If there is a single problem with homebasing business, it is the inability to set a just return for your work (markup). Value yourself!

Keystone. If you decide to sell wholesale to the stores, remember to arrive at a retail price; most stores keystone (double the wholesale price). An artist consulted with me about marketing the exquisite hand-painted silk kimonos she had made. She wanted to sell them to boutiques and department stores. Labor (hers), fabric, sewing (an assistant), dyes, and overhead totaled $150. They would have to retail for $295 (buyers generally mark uneven numbers). Now the question is . . . would the customer pay $295 for a kimono even though it is a work of art. One thing I have to keep in mind always . . . not to judge what someone else can afford by my pocketbook. Yes, there was a market for her product. She, also, retails to individuals herself, being careful not to undercut the store's price.

Food Products. Are you planning to market your highly touted cheese- or carrot cakes, cookies, or chili con carne? Food specialty products are sold both to restaurants and to individual customers. Advice given by the experienced about

---

*that "worker" may be you.

pricing is to triple the costs of the ingredients. Figure one-third for ingredients, one-third for time, and one-third for profit and overhead. This is the price to restaurants; for your private customers, charge more. Depending on the affluence of the community, prices will vary in different parts of the country. Prices are based also on what the customer will pay and availability.

Get Small Business Administration Publication #193, consult with an adviser from their SCORE program, your accountant, and talk to store buyers for feedback. For sure, they will tell you if your wholesale price is too high.

If you plan to use a distributor to mass-market your product to grocery chains, the pricing structure changes and increases in cost. Add about 30 percent for distributor costs to your wholesale price, plus 20 to 30 percent for the grocers' profit. Now the final retail price is determined.

As an example, let's say you have added up the costs of ingredients, outside labor (food manufacturer), overhead, packaging, and the cost totals $2.00 per item. Then add 30 percent percent for your profit.

$2.00	cost per item
.60	your profit—30 percent of cost
$2.60	price to distributor
.78	distributor's markup based on 30 percent
$3.38	wholesale price to grocers
1.01	grocers' markup based on 30 percent
$4.39	retail cost per item

Will the customer pay $4.39 for the product? If not, can the cost to make the products be cut without changing the quality; is your price based on buying in quantity, ingredients, and packaging items?

Payroll. No need to tell you to pay your employees well. The London *Sunday Times* reports that an American designer pays older British citizens $10 to $27 to knit sweaters he sells in the U.S. for $400! The paper published a picture of an older woman holding one of those sweaters that took two days to knit. In London, it sells for $290 after markup and taxes, on a wholesale price of $130. Now in the U.S. the sweater retails for $400, and wholesales for about $185. The designer justifies the disparity between the $44 cost of each sweater and the selling price because of the London agent's commission, shipping charges to the U.S., 30 percent import duty and handling charges.

Shades of the old sweatshops—low, low wages. Another of those old sayings that carries the message. . . . "If you pay peanuts, then hire monkeys." And if you are an employed "monkey," change your diet. Say good-bye to the boss.

Protection

> *It is not true life is one damn thing after another—it's one damn thing over and over.*
>
> —Edna St. Vincent Millay

Insurance. Protect your investment. You may want to take your chances, but a rider on your present Homeowner policy (for product liability, business equipment, fire and theft) costs $50 to $100 and is a small investment for peace of mind. Investigate food liability insurance if you are dealing in food products.

There's personal liability to protect you as an individual. Again, if this coverage is not included in your Homeowner's policy, get it. It costs little for maximum coverage and frees you from worry. That same energy used for worrying can be used more constructively in your business. Tell your insurance agent that you have a homebased business and what kind of a business you operate, whether clients or customers come to your home, merchandise stored, and any other pertinent disclosure.

Still you can prevent problems. Just because you know to sidestep that wedge in the driveway doesn't mean a stranger will—so fix it. Do not store materials used in business too close to water heaters, furnaces, or stoves. Storing heavy equipment or merchandise in the attic can undermine the ceilings. Also, remember that basements have been known to flood.

Automobile Insurance. Assuming you do have adequate coverage; however, do employees who use their cars for your business? You can obtain "nonowned auto liability."

Workmen's Compensation. This coverage provides benefits to employees for on-the-job injuries regardless of whose fault it is.

Insurance Poor. We all know about that. Buy enough insurance and compare rates of the different companies. Some other kinds of coverage for the self-employed: Partnership, Disability, Medical, Income-Business Interruption, Travel.

Copyright. Definition: *A copyright gives the owner the right to exclude others from reproducing his or her work without specific permission and/or payment.* Creative work takes the form of literary works: books, articles, poems, plays, paintings, musical compositions, choreography, illustrations, sculpture, tapes, and records . . . just about anything.

The government is your best friend, recognizes that you are the sole owner and only you have rights to sell, distribute, or reproduce copies of your work to prepare derivative works, and to perform or display publicly whatever it is you have had copyrighted. Under a new 1978 law, protection lasts for the life of the creator plus fifty years (the "plus years" are for your heirs or as your will states).

Many people think that sending a description of the idea or a copy of a manuscript through registered mail back to themselves in the dated envelope left unopened is *sufficient* protection. It isn't. It costs so little to copyright; write or call for further information to Copyright Office, c/o Library of Congress, Washington, D.C. 20231.

Patent. Definition: *To secure exclusive right to make, use, or sell a product or a process.* It is important to consult a patent attorney, and it takes time to get it. If you want to have your idea evaluated, the Small Business Publication #91, *Ideas into Dollars*, describes this phase after the initial idea has been created:

Idea Evaluation Phase

Idea evaluation is the first major step after a concrete, detailed idea has been developed. This is a critical phase since every following phase requires the investment of more time and money. The purpose of an idea evaluation is to determine the overall technical and commercial feasibility of an idea—what its full potential actually is.

These evaluation activities seek to determine whether the fledgling invention is a marked improvement over its competition; whether it is likely to be commercially via-

58

ble; what the probable demand for it will be; who could produce it; and how it would be distributed. The ultimate purpose here is to arrive at the decision to go ahead to the commercialization stage, to redesign the invention, or to kill the project altogether.

The same publication lists several University Evaluation Centers (the costs appear to be nominal), Government Evaluation Offices, publications, Inventors' Associations, and other organizations for protection and legal assistance.

Keep your idea to yourself until you find out how to protect it. You do not have to build a prototype or practice the process to get an idea evaluated or patented. Writing the idea down on numbered pages in a bound notebook, signed and dated, witnessed by someone you trust is a first step to take. (See Resources.)

Trademark. Definition: *The brand name of a given product, or service, or the symbol by which the product or symbol is known.* Apply only for state protection if your business will be confined to your state. Contact the State Department of Commerce or the Secretary of State for information. If you wish to use your trademark nationally, applications are made to the U.S. Patent and Trademark Office, Washington, D.C. 20231. A consultation with a patent attorney would advise you if a trademark search is indicated.

Royalty. Definition: *A payment made to an author, composer, or designer for each copy of his/her work sold or to an inventor for each article sold under a patent.* I know you keep reading in this book to consult an attorney or an accountant but it is better to obtain guidance beforehand than to wish that you had. Creative people may not be as interested in the business of their art as they are in the process of creating. Too many have been victims of exploitation, innocently signing away their rights or receiving too little monetary return for their work. Don't let it happen to you.

Promotion

*Of course I'm a publicity **hound**. Aren't all crusaders? How can you accomplish anything unless people know what you are trying to do?*

—Vivian Kellems

THE WAYS TO SELL YOUR WARES

There's no such thing as a "shy" business. A couple of women spoke to me after one of the seminars, and asked if I knew of any business for people who were "shy." It's difficult to be an entrepreneur and assertiveness does help. Learning to be assertive is a skill that can be acquired like any other. But if you have a product that needs to be shown to store buyers and you just can't find the courage, try to get a sales representative.

Sales Representative. Hire a sales representative to call on stores on a regular basis. Unless you have an extensive line and can provide the representative with a good living, they usually represent more than one line, covering a specific geographical area.

How to find one? Look in the yellow pages of the telephone book, under Sales Representatives. Call the merchandise marts for recommendations. Put an ad for a salesperson in a trade publication. Ask store buyers or representatives for recommendations. Go to the trade shows and seek out a representative.

A sales representative's salary is 10 to 20 percent of the wholesale sales. They submit the orders to you and you do the billing, shipping, and collecting.

Finding a good representative is no easy task.

Large cities such as New York, Chicago, and Los Angeles have resident buying offices, each representing different groups of department stores across the nation. They send out bulletins of new merchandise to their accounts, show buyers a display of new lines in their offices, and will take buyers to the manufacturers.

There's an anecdote about salesmanship that goes like this.

> "Two shoe salespersons were sent to Africa. One wired home that it was hopeless, for none of the natives wore shoes. The other wired back that it was the biggest unexplored market in existence."

An enthusiastic salesperson is what you need and that person may very well be you.

A successful weaver of women's clothing told me she would not let anyone else "rep" her line but herself because nobody can discuss the beauty of the intricacies like she can. She has acquired 255 accounts nationwide by displaying her clothes at major trade shows twice a year. Remember, buyers are always looking for new merchandise. Their job depends on it. You can show the products that you make, or have made for you, or lines you represent to store buyers and resident buyers. Call first and make an appointment. If you live too far away, send samples by mail with return postage guaranteed.

ON CONSIGNMENT

Many arts-and-crafts products and books are placed in galleries and shops on consignment. This means the owner will display your merchandise and pay when it is sold. Sometimes it is the only way to obtain visibility. Have a signed invoice for the merchandise you leave. If the articles are breakable, include an agreement of responsibility for damages. Once the product proves itself by selling, the buyer usually will purchase outright. You have the prerogative of changing your terms for consignment to outright sale.

MAIL ORDER

Mail order business is fun. The mailbox becomes a slot machine—unpredictable. Some days there are handfuls of orders, other days—lemons. A tricky enterprise.

Consumers made 15 percent of their purchases by mail in 1985. Sales by mail will rise to about $35 billion, or about 11.5 percent of general merchandise sales, according to the Direct Mail/Marketing Association, a New York-based Trade group.

Selling by mail order is another way to market a single product or many. The product or products can be your own or somebody else's. A "leader" item is sometimes used to get customers to send for a catalog of other items you are selling. This is a way to develop a mailing list.

It is important to find the appropriate media. Newspapers and magazines are for the smaller entrepreneur. Radio and television may not be suitable or affordable.

It may be possible to get free editorial plugs. Call on an editor (by appointment); send a picture of the merchandise or a sample to the shopping editor of a newspaper or magazine. To get the name of the right editor, sift through magazines at the library or newsstands. Don't count on getting the merchandise back. Guarantee cost of return shipment. Even so, the percentage of return of samples is low. Chalk the investment up to advertising. Follow up with a call or a letter to find out when it will be featured or to request its return.

Here are a few products applicable to mail order to trigger your imagination: animal products, health remedies, books, mail order courses, green thumb supplies, furniture, specialty foods, kitchen gadgets, games, gags, fads, coins, stamps, clothing, jewelry, tools, and good luck objects. (See Resources.)

CATALOGS

A costly venture but can pay off nicely. Critique those you receive. Are the products available in your own neighborhood; are they less expensive; are they more unusual? In my files I have a collection of catalogs from all parts of the world; Irish imports from Shannon, French perfumes, gourmet food products, all-cotton merchandise, discount vitamins, museum gallery gifts. . . . Not all the items have to be stocked. Many catalogers stock a small amount of each item or none at all, purchasing from the manufacturer as orders are received. This is not a business to enter lightly. Do your homework.

DIRECT MAIL—FOR PRODUCTS OR SERVICES

Although mailing lists are available for purchase, you can develop your own by simply using membership lists of organizations to which you belong, telephone books, trade directories, business cards you have collected over the years, your friends' friends, and so on. If your product has a specialized audience, such as an article suitable for collectors of antique toys or trains, then purchase a reliable, up-to-date mailing list for that target population.

I have used both methods—bought mailing lists and used my own list gathered by the methods mentioned above. Expect a return of 10 percent—and be pleased if it's 20 percent. A mailing has a long life expectancy. Don't be surprised if you receive a request for the product three years later.

The mailer itself can be a postcard, circular, leaflet, reprint, stuffer, or discount coupon. Include an order blank within the format whenever a product is to be purchased.

Make it look professional. If the layout and design are beyond your talents, use a designer and a printer who specialize in direct mail. If your budget allows, furnish the address labels and they will handle the mailing.

Use whatever system (color code, key chart) that will feed back to you the pulling power of each mailing. It becomes doubly important to make sure purchased mailing lists are really up-to-date. People do move around without leaving a forwarding address. People do die and companies do go out of business.

Lists you purchase may not be appropriate for the type of business you establish or they may have been used by so many companies that they are overworked. Consider how much mail you receive and throw away without a glance at its contents. Compare the features of mailers that caught your attention in the past.

FLEA MARKETS AND FAIRS

Going to the regularly scheduled monthly flea markets has become a national sport. Friends of mine brag about their latest acquisitions, schedule their lives around the eventful date, the first Sunday of the month is "wouldn't miss it for the world" Flea Day.

It is an inexpensive way to market-test your product for selling price and consumer response. There're waiting lists for space at some of the better-known fairs and markets. (See Resources.) It is a place where parents teach their children how to shop, compare price, and bargain; eavesdrop the next time you see a father whispering in his child's ear how to respond to the bicycle vendor.

STREET VENDORS

Is there anyone left in this country who has not held one or stopped at one. In Los Angeles, it would seem that every sidewalk, lawn, garage, freeway exit, along with vacant lots, parts of gasoline stations, street corners, arcades are filled with street vendors. They comprise Saturday and Sunday moonlighters to full-timers selling luggage, used and new clothing, jewelry, furniture, bric-a-brac, flowers, shoes, bags of oranges, fruits and vegetables from the backs of pickup trucks, bridge tables, and front lawn displays. It's becoming a coast-to-coast bazaar, as colorful and lively as the most ancient street markets of Istanbul. And it's an honorable way of making a living.

HOME PARTIES

An easy way to open a business. . . . in someone else's living room. The merchandise sold can be made by you or by an established company. Multilevel marketing is a designation that usually indicates three levels of selling: the distributor, the sales manager, and the sales reps. The products range from health, cosmetics, housecleaning, toys, to the latest entry, computers.

The party hostess loans house and retinue of friends and

relatives for a gift and sometimes percentage of the sales. (See Resources.)

Two seminar students now have a very successful home-party business selling quality children's toys. They bought their merchandise quite cautiously in the beginning to determine which toys would sell and to keep their capital investment within their capabilities. A year and a half later they have a warehouse of stock, have hired reps, are solidly booked for the next holiday season, and are planning to manufacture their own line of toys. A fringe benefit—for holidays and birthdays they can select toys for their own young children from their warehouse.

NO-COST OR LOW-COST PROMOTION AND PUBLICITY FOR SERVICES AND PRODUCTS

There are many ways to promote or publicize your product or service without spending exorbitant sums of money. It takes as much effort to establish a market for an inexpensive product as it does for a costly one. Utilize this checklist *before* investing in the cost of advertising.

- Tell every family member about your new business. Families can be a great broadcast system. Word of mouth will bring some customers to your doorstep.
- Tell all your friends and associates.
- Mention the service or show the product to all the tradespeople you deal with. If it's wearable, wear it!
- Do you have attractive business cards and matching stationery? A well-designed letterhead on quality paper reflects your service or talent. Carry your business cards with you always and give them out at every opportunity.

  There's a new twist, new to the U.S. but not to the Japanese, to the information on a business card. It can resemble a condensed résumé printed on one or both sides.

  Another consideration—can the design of the card reflect what kind of business it is? A fiber artist's card looks and feels like cloth: an illustrator has a caricature of himself holding a paintbrush on one side of his calling card.
- If a prepared résumé is helpful in promoting your service or product, make it professional in content and appear-

65

ance. Résumé writing is trendy, so be sure your format is today's.
- Print a flier for neighborhood door-to-door distribution. Put the fliers on cars in parking lots. Post signs on trees.
- Check with the phone company to see if your phone number can tie in with your service or product. Example: 000-GIFT is the number used by a home business that selects gifts for companies and individuals. List your business in the yellow pages.
- Purchase an answering machine or an answering service.
- Send a "Who, What, When, and How" press release to the local newspapers. Make it newsworthy—something that makes your service or product original.
- Send a leaflet, letter, postcard, or order blank to a mailing list of potential consumers. Remember, a 10 percent return is considered good!
- Arrange to speak to organizations or college classes about an interesting facet of your service, and/or demonstrate your craft or product.
- Old-fashioned sandwich boards (walking billboards) are making a fashionable return to the advertising scene. It's unique, inexpensive, and causes talk, which is exactly what you want.
- Join organizations that will give you professional exposure.
- Exhibit your craft or product in trade shows and fairs. This should keep you busy; there are about six thousand fairs and festivals each year.
- Donate a sample of your craft or product (if not too costly for you) to fund-raisers and benefits. Ask for a receipt for tax records.
- Have holiday sales.
- Assemble a press kit, which includes an autobiography, or your résumé; the history and uniqueness of your company or service; your picture ($8'' \times 10''$). Send to target newspapers. Call one week after the press kit has been received. If no response is forthcoming, follow up with other releases.
- Contact the program directors, consumer media, television and radio and magazine editors. Send your press kit.
- Teach a class at home, at a college or university, adult education at high schools, at Y.M.C.A.'s, churches, or temples.

- Buy sweatshirts and uniforms for the little league teams with the name of your business imprinted.
- Give your business a birthday party and invite your clients.
- If you know the birthdays of customers' children, send congratulations.
- Write a newsletter to send to clients. The trick companies use is to mention everything under the sun except their service or product.
- Order a giveaway with your company name: ballpoint pens, T-shirts, key rings, bookmarks, miniature notepads, calendars. Keep your name in front of the consumer.
- Put up a sign, *if permissible*, in front of your location. Hang a sign on your car or on the car of anyone else who will let you.
- Have labels made to attach to your product.
- Try the "free plug" for your product. Select appropriate magazines or newspapers that feature new items and mail a sample with complete details, material, price, delivery terms. Do not expect your samples to be returned. It's worth the try. Magazines will give an editorial review when you purchase an ad. Ask for one.
- Read, clip, and file articles that give information about merchandising, marketing, resources, and anything that is helpful now or in the future.
- Join with local businesses who send discount coupons to residents.
- Classified ads in newspapers and magazines are more affordable than display ads.
- "Cold calling" is selling by calling on or phoning people you don't know and have no previous contact with, usually phone numbers picked from telephone books or going door-to-door.
- Write an article about some angle of what you do or who you are. Submit to publications for consideration.
- Exhibit your craft at the neighborhood bank.
- Give unexpected follow-up service to customers via a phone call, a present, or a note. Thoughtfulness in business dealings today is so unusual, customers will be added to the ranks of your broadcast system.
- And don't forget to thank customers for each referral.

With lots of hard work these publicity ideas will enable you to advertise for little or no cost. Keep in mind that your endeavors may not show an immediate payoff.

Devote some time each and every day to promote your service or product.

If your budget can afford display advertising in magazines and newspapers, familiarize yourself with copywriting and ad design, marketing techniques. Learn how to select the best medium or hire a good consultant.

Persistence

When YOU stop, so does the business.
—BNF

The development of any business, regardless of where it is based, demands persistence. To become a successful home-based entrepreneur requires a *double* dose of persistence! True entrepreneurs *have* that necessary drive, that sustained effort, to realize the success of *the idea*. They persevere!

Are entrepreneurs born with that success trait? *The Wall Street Journal* reports that research has found only three groups that have produced a remarkably high number of entrepreneurs. Of these, only one group can be credited with this drive as a "birthright"—the sons of Mormon second marriages!

The other two groups are Vietnam refugees and hippies. Vietnamese who have immigrated to this country are noted for their industry—working two or three jobs almost around the clock to accumulate a nest egg to open their own business. No personal sacrifice is too great for the entire family in order to achieve this goal.

A former hippie, who is now a millionaire, began his herbal tea company picking the ingredients that grew wild in the Colorado hills. The names he chose for the different brews have a distinctively hippie flavor that arouses the consumer's curiosity. How does "Red Zinger" strike you? I know I had to try it.

If you are neither a hippie, nor a Vietnamese refugee, nor even a child of a Mormon's second marriage, there's still a chance for you to succeed.

A group of self-made millionaires who were interviewed attributed their achievements to their persistence in finding a way out of poverty. Seeing and envying the way in which people with money live, they decided there was nothing to

69

lose by taking risks. In taking action to change their lives, *risking failure* was in itself considered by them an accomplishment.

How these people relate their concepts of entrepreneurship to their own success has been adapted to the following self-assessment test. The correct responses are really quite apparent.

A SELF-ASSESSMENT TEST

Yes	No	
____	____	Do you need more money?
____	____	Are you achievement-oriented?
____	____	Are you willing to take risks?
____	____	Are you willing to work hard?
____	____	You may be willing to work hard, but are you energetic?
____	____	Are you optimistic? It certainly helps when there are business lulls, problems to solve, and mistakes to recover from.
____	____	Are you an extrovert or are you willing to learn how to be an extrovert when it comes to marketing? In salesmanship, modesty will not pay off.
____	____	Do you enjoy learning new skills?
____	____	Are transitions easy for you? Company president one minute—then cook for the kids—regain the presidency—change the baby's diaper . . .
____	____	Have you known job displacement (a euphemism for "layoff") when you felt secure in that job?
____	____	Do you have a well-developed sense of humor?
____	____	Can you make your own "luck"?

With hard work, experience, and money it would be difficult not to be successful. People have achieved what they want without money, even without prior experience, but rarely without hard work.

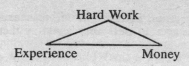

Hard Work

Experience   Money

Industries have developed incentive programs based on research about increasing the workers' productivity and re-establishing the work ethic. The work ethic, they say, builds character. My research about how to get work out of me shows that I need my own incentive program, plenty of concrete rewards.

I grew up with a reward system and a roomful of curly haired dolls to show for it. My working widowed mother found it expedient to change my behavior with a promise of a long, curly haired (mine was straight and short, of course) doll.

Persistence or perseverance deserves frequent rewards. Because it is a difficult trait to develop, it needs to be reinforced often. It has taken a reward system of many "dolls," cookies, chocolates, gallons of ice cream, apple pies (you can tell I'm really into health foods) to keep me on target. Small missions accomplished are also rewarded with my own pats on my back.

A reward of jogging at the beach is to one person what playing bridge or going to a movie is to another. Find your own ways to reward yourself for every accomplishment. The reward system does work. Its success depends on tuning in to what you consider a reward.

For small-size accomplishments such as letter writing, business meetings, telephoning, give yourself small-size rewards—food, walks, gardening breaks, or even taking the garbage out if this is an activity that you happen to enjoy. For middle-size accomplishments such as the completion of an article, a class, a business phone call that takes more "guts" than most, give yourself a middle-size reward—an afternoon off, a nap, a new blouse or shirt. For the big effort, accomplishment, achievement, go for a big reward—a trip, the purchase of something you don't need, whatever fills the bill for you. Right now, I'm going to pick my reward for finishing this book—airplane tickets to Europe!

Sometimes the accomplished goals are not commensurate with the effort put out for them. No matter, give them equal rewards. What renews me is a "cease-fire" of perseverance, getting completely away from business. Then when I return, I am eager to persevere again. For some people, perseverance is an inborn trait and no coaxing, no rewards are necessary. Imagine that! To other people, *perseverance* has puritanical connotations, sounds too serious and humorless.

To overcome the fear and anxiety of a large business goal, set small goals for each day. Attaining a one-a-day goal will give you a sense of accomplishment. Let that good feeling prevail! It generates more energy and a successful feeling about yourself, which lead to the continuation of goal-setting and accomplishments.

Personal success is exhilarating. When those self-made millionaires were asked why they continued to work so hard when they had attained all the money they needed, they concurred that in the beginning they worked for money, then for the excitement, and now it is a game—the pleasure of exercising success itself.

There is pleasure and satisfaction in getting an idea, developing it, and seeing it through to actuality. So many home businesses began as embryos and look at them babies now!

"IF IT'S TO BE IT'S UP TO ME."

Problems of Success

*I simply don't see the point of getting up
at six all the time you are young and
working eighteen hours a day in order to
be a millionaire, and then when you are
a millionaire still getting up at six and
working eighteen hours a day. . . .*
—Nancy Mitford

What are you complaining about? You worked hard, developed a successful business, the money's good, so what's the problem?

To Move or not to Move. The business has outgrown the home: either the business moves out or you do. The enticement of a HBB was the luxury of working home and now a choice has to be made. Choosing to set a cap on business growth and stay put is one solution. And that's the decision many of us who prefer the home-work setting make.

Entrepreneurs who may have chosen to begin at home, mainly because of small capital investment, look forward to the split. So for some, it's no problem but timing. How much backup capital is necessary to afford a separate place of business? It's said "If someone has to ask how much it costs to own a yacht, then he's not ready to own one." Both questions are similar. A year's operating capital tucked away in reserve is the recommendation of a business management adviser.

Delegating. Another major problem is the trouble that comes when the business has survived the start-up phase and has outgrown the hands-on, one-person management that worked so well in the early stages. Now the owner has to redefine his/her role in the company if it is to continue to grow. Day-to-day details are time-consuming, leaving little time to plan for future, to look for new opportunities. There's no way for a business to grow if you continue to do it all yourself. Hire assistants who will take over the tasks that give you no satisfaction, or those chores that others could do as well or better than you.

Fast Track. When the business took off before you were ready, now that's a problem. You're overwhelmed . . . which? what! how? Confusion— In planning the business include some "what if's" because overnight success is not a fairy tale. It happens.

Business Comes First. To love what you do and feel that it matters is fine but when the business is ALL that matters, problems may arise. Health, difficulties with family relationships, loss of objectivity are common to enterprising, business-comes-first personalities. Set priorities.

Money Matters

*When I was young I used to think money
was the most important thing in life; now
that I am old, I know it is.*

—Oscar Wilde

CAPITAL

Where does the money come from? *The Wall Street Journal*
reports that most people reach into their own pockets for
start-up cash. Half of 1,597 business owners surveyed used
personal savings; one in twenty resorted to personal loans,
using a home for collateral. Demonstrating a demand for
the product can be adequate evidence to convince the bank
to give a loan. We used our advance orders for the "Octo-
Puss" to secure a loan from the bank to purchase large
quantities of yarn.

Business Plan. Prepare a detailed business plan to raise
capital. Family, friends, and even strangers may be interested in loaning money for start-up. Enthusiasm is convincing and contagious. Show a willingness to commit your own
financial resources . . . if you have some.

The basic components of the plan include:

The Product. A description of the product or service, the
need it satisfies; identify the potential user, how and where
it is to be manufactured, assessment of competition, and
why the product is better.

Marketing Projection. Explain how your product or service is to be sold, who will buy it, the advertising and promotion program to announce the business. If clients or customers have made advance commitments to buy your product, mention that here.

People. Work biographies or résumés of you and your partners, if any.

Financial Projection. Cash-flow statement is a forecast of the cash a business expects to receive and disburse during a given period of time. How can you project sales and income when you haven't begun your business? Making these projections shows that the entrepreneur is going to try to do at least that amount. You can show potential growth of the business on three sets of sales assumptions—low, expected, and better-than-expected.

Your business plan should be neatly typed and packaged in a folder or ring binder. Present the plan verbally, in person, to your banker or potential investor.

Some reputable schools have MBA students who will advise you how to make a business proposal, for little or no fee.

The Small Business Administration (SBA) is another resource for capital and lots of advice. Many booklets are printed on a variety of topics related to starting and conducting a business. A group of retired business executives (SCORE) volunteer their time at the local SBA offices to answer phone inquiries and arrange for personal counseling.

Risk-taking is a large factor in every business venture. For shoestring wallets, it is the only way to get started. An Arabic word for *risk* translates as *earning one's daily bread*.

CASH FLOW

The little guy who can least afford to wait gets paid last. A San Francisco caterer put on a successful party for a corporate client, submitted her bill for $3,500 and received nothing for ninety days. Finally, the corporate controller sent $500 and offered installment payments of $500 a month, which did not include the interest penalty for late payment.

"It's in the mail," "You're next to be paid," "The book-keeper is out sick," or "It must be lost in the mail—we'll put a stopper on that check and issue another." Become familiar with these responses because the song is the same, just the lyrics are different. Even the federal government pays small-business bills last of all. A recent two-year survey of selected federal agencies showed that of those bills paid late (as long as seven months late), 90 percent were owed to small businesses.

What can you do about it? First, expect that collections may be slow, and second, try to avoid charge accounts.

Some store operations are so small that they use the money return from the sales of your merchandise for working capital, while you sit on your accounts payable. But most people who don't pay just don't have the money.

Cash-on-Delivery is now a common practice. Doctors, dentists, plumbers, and electricians practically go through your wallet beforehand and are not at all shy about it. When selling to smaller stores, it is not unusual to sell on a C.O.D. basis. It is safer with some stores because of their under-capitalization and their day-to-day operation. They may be here today and gone tomorrow.

Large department stores will not accept C.O.D. orders. Be prepared—they, too, can take several months to pay their accounts. When your working capital is short, it is not always easy to hang in there, expecially when there are too many accounts overdue. A phone call sometimes gives the necessary prod to have a heart-to-heart talk with the company's computer or who's in charge.

An incentive for prompt payment is 2 percent off the amount due if the bill is paid within ten days upon receipt of delivery. You may find that customers disregard the "ten days upon receipt" and discount 2 percent upon payment in thirty days.

Another solution is to assess interest on late payments, commonly 1.5 percent a month after thirty days. However, many customers may refuse to pay the charge.

Those who provide a regular and recurring service, such as advertising and public relations firms, usually charge monthly retainers.

If you offer a onetime service, ask for advance deposits of 50 percent and the rest on completion of the job.

No contract business should be concluded on a handshake

alone. Even if the client is your father, put the terms in writing. A written contract has many advantages besides protecting you in case of disagreements or misunderstandings later on as to what was initially agreed to. It can be helpful to you in planning a project or a delivery to have a clear description of what the client or customer expects.

What's in a Name?

Plenty!
—BNF

If your name is Mary Jane Smythington-North or Theodore (Teddy) Hummingbird IV, don't use it for your business's name. Picking a name is a tough assignment. It has exasperated the largest of corporations. In fact, there is a company in San Francisco that does nothing else but find names. They charge $7,000 to $10,000 to develop a single company or product name. This should convince you that naming your business is an important consideration. Here are some rules to remember:

- Choose a name that advertises the service provided, such as "George's Secretarial Service." The kind of business determines whether using your own name may be too limiting. But if you are known in the community, it can be helpful, or if you just want to see your name in lights, go ahead.
- Choose a name that people can pronounce. This has been the rule. A new Japanese car was deliberately given an unpronounceable name for advertising purposes. But the corporation has a million dollar (you don't) ad campaign capitalizing on the funny-sounding name.
- Choose a name that describes the product. It is advisable to spare the consumer guesswork, thus saving small businesses valuable start-up capital and time. For example, *The Arts and Crafts Company* says more than *The Company*. A name like The Company is usually chosen to serve as an umbrella name for different enterprises.

- The longer the name, the greater the cost in advertising space and the more difficult it is to remember.
- Sound out your friends or a consultant to get their reactions to the name. Their responses may make you have second thoughts about your selection. Live with it awhile. See it in print.
- Listings in the telephone directory (White and Yellow Pages) are in alphabetical order. If the competition is negligible, it makes no difference, but if there are fifty competitors' names ahead of yours, you may want to play the "A" game.

MAKING IT LEGAL

Legalizing the name is a simple process. If the name is other than your own, file a fictitious name statement, called a DBA (Doing Business As). At your local city hall there is an alphabetical registry of all fictitious names you can check to see if someone else has already laid claim to your choice. The keeper of names in California is a little-known resource called the Office of Name Availability, in the Secretary of State's office, where harried clerks receive nine hundred calls per day from companies searching for corporate names.

If you are going to operate in a small city and have no plans to expand, you may not need to have a name registration search. But if there are big plans in the future, there are companies that charge about $300 for a company name search, which includes examining a computerized list of four million names, seventy-five telephone directories from major cities, and sixty other directories of names.

Mind Your Own Business

Don't agonize. Organize.
The biggest sin is sitting on your ass.
— Florynce R. Kennedy

If you have read thus far and are rarin' to mind your own business, then you are the very reader I imagined. If an idea has germinated, so much the better. But don't fret if you still can't come up with what you would like to do. The very fact that you are interested is the beginning and mulling over the pros and cons of one idea over another eventually will bring you to something you want to try.

Don't be a window-shopper, one of those people who look and look and look and never take the leap. Have you ever said, "Remember when I had that very same idea two years ago?" when you saw someone else's success? Nothing comes to sleepers but a dream.

Few people think up an idea that is wholly new and original. The person who takes an idea, one of a kind or not, and runs with it is the one who will get it launched. Business ideas can be based on a new product or service or "the better mousetrap" concept—you know a better way.

Some people get stymied in life because they care too much what other people will think of them and their "crazy" ideas. They were probably the same as children—afraid to speak out in class. And if you grew up in the era when "look before you leap" was the rule, remember that in spite of many indicators that a business idea of yours is a shaky undertaking, enthusiasm, determination, and hard work (a holistic approach to HBB) can reverse the prognosis.

Mark Twain said: *"There are two times in a man's life*

when he should not speculate; when he can't afford it and when he can.''

I disagree. "Speculation" and risk-taking are the only ways up and out of being poor, doing what you want and taking responsibility for that action, and adventuring through life. For moonlighters who can afford to "speculate," it has been the best way to unwind after a hard day on the job and/ or a springboard to a new business. What a sweet decision to have (the opportunity) to make in your lifetime a full-time job and part-time entrepreneur, or no other job besides full-time entrepreneur.

Are moonlighters workaholics? Perhaps some are, but not if you consider *work* as your *sport* or *hobby*. Others may choose tennis, racketball, partying, watching television. Moonlighters like *profitable hobbies*.

Entrepreneurship means that it's okay and even admirable to be constantly changing or adding on enterprises. It is the nature of entrepreneurship to risk, to change.

When your business succeeds, so does your status and income. Working for someone else is often a waiting game— waiting for the boss to acknowledge your creative contributions, for a promotion, for more money. You don't get rich working for others and you may discover you don't automatically get rich working for yourself, either. But corporate ball-playing and turning the other cheek too many times—all for the sake of corporate harmony—can cause personnal, physical, and emotional disharmony.

Homebased businesses and entrepreneurship go hand in hand. It's a creative process. A business can be seen to develop from beginning to end. *Making it grow*—how many people can say that about what they do?

If the decision is to go after an HBB (our new degree), always remember the Homebased Business Entrepreneur's oath:

"I am working for myself. I am the boss and the employee. To make a success of this business I must run, not walk, and if I come to a halt, so does my business. If I do it later, I'll earn it later. I am on my way."

Introduction to Different Homebased Businesses Offering Products or Services

In the following sections you will find numerous ideas for your homebased business. I compiled the businesses from five sources: correspondence with people who write me from all over the United States, Europe, Asia, and even Africa; homebased businesses featured in newspapers and magazines; services or products generated from a home base that I personally use as a customer; from clients in my practice as a business consultant; and from participants in the seminars I teach.

Whatever you decide to do, keep in mind that launching a business is a major step and a lot of work; however, sustaining it is equally important. Although most of us wish our business would be an overnight success—it can happen, but more than likely you will be like the rest of us—it will take time. Not six weeks or six months. Two years is more realistic for a fledgling business to become a thriving endeavor. And that's if you work at it diligently.

Looking back, you will remember going into your own business was a little scary. For me, as well as for others, it's worth all the hard work to be doing what you want to do. So look out, there's more fun and adventure ahead.

Now when you browse through the following pages, look for an idea that feels right for you. The sections are divided into two parts: the first part lists businesses that involve *Products*, the second part deals with *Services*.

1. *Products* made by you and/or purchased from someone else for resale.

   Each of us is a consumer, more or less. Things we ordinarily made ourselves, we now buy from someone else. Individual entrepreneurs are selling products people didn't even know they needed fifteen years ago. Check your closet, refrigerator, kitchen, and the rest of your environment. How many of those products did you make? The other day when I complained that it is impossible to open up any packaged item, including empty plastic market vegetable bags and the embalmed cracker packages, the clerk asked, "Don't you have one of those package openers? There's an electric gadget that attaches to the wall . . ." Terrific! I haven't yet succumbed to the food processor, the microwave oven, the trash compactor. All the pushbuttons on my ten-year-old dryer are still unfriendly.

2. *Services* you can provide.

   Today, among the self-employed, the expansion of the service sector has risen to 78 percent. The demand for services has risen accordingly, mainly because of present economic factors. Busy working couples need a "wife" and the "wife" needs a replacement for the (handy) man around the house. More home duties are relegated to outside help. Small firms need experts, too, from engineering to finance and it is far less expensive to engage an outside consultant than to have one on a full-time salary. In a depressed economy businesses terminate full-time experts, for example, escrow and loan officers and appraisers, and engage them as the need arises. The explosive growth of the fields of communications, health, and entertainment, to name a few, has opened up new careers for the self-employed.

Please note:

- In classifying kinds of businesses, sometimes it is difficult to determine whether an activity is a service or a product

or both. No matter . . . you will find it under one section or the other.
- Some businesses are self-explanatory and, therefore, have minimal or no comment; others include more description because of their unusual nature, their relative newness, the public interest they generate, their easy startup, and/or the low investment they may require.
- Anticipated earnings are omitted because too many variables affect a homebased business's potential: geography, population, seasonal demand, quality, competition, and varying amounts of profit or markup.
- Some of these businesses are strictly homebased, suitable for the true homebody, and others require outside contact as well.
- For those of you who already have a business in mind, check the lists of businesses to see if there's a companion business that can fit in. Remember *diversifying*? Services and products can also be combined.
- I purposely included unusual ideas to help you stretch your imagination. I believe you will find some surprises ahead in what constitutes a business.

The Home as a Product

*Radio, sewing machine, book ends,
ironing board and that great big piano
lamp—peace, that's what I like.*
—Eudora Welty

BED AND BREAKFAST

The best example of putting the spare room in your home
to work is the growing demand by United States tourists for
"bed and breakfast" shelter rather than local hotels or mo-
tels. Accommodations range from town house apartments
to Victorian homes, in residential or downtown areas. Britons have long used bed and breakfast dwellings. The idea
spread to the Continent, and now is catching on in the
United States.

Actually, it has been an age-old custom here, better known
as: "guest home," "tourist room," "room to let,"
"rooming house," or "lodgers." These are the signs that
have hung on private houses for years. Guesthouses are popular because travel costs have risen 50 percent faster than
the consumer price index. Hotel rooms are $80 and more
per night. Compare that to $16 to $65 for your spare room,
topped off by your special breakfast recipes. Tourists like
to meet the "natives" and some homeowners enjoy the contact of interesting people—a kind of foreign exchange.

"All the comforts of home" are offered by nearly five
thousand guesthouses across the country, which are listed
in associations of guesthouses. Countless other homeowners
operate independently. Lists are obtainable from directory

publishers, newspaper travel editors, travel agents, libraries, and automobile clubs.

In addition to travelers, consider taking into your home a foreign or out-of-state student. Call the local university and college to list your house as an available accommodation.

BED AND BREAKFAST DIRECTORIES

As a spin-off, the work of putting together the lists of accommodations is a business in its own right. One directory started up because a traveler became so enthusiastic about her experience with the bed and board network in England that, on returning to the United States, she placed ads in magazines for hosts. The geographical area was limited and specialized in one particular region. Each candidate host's home was inspected before permission was granted to join the league and advertise in the directory at a cost of $55 per family. Do you have a directory for your area? (See Resources.)

BED AND BREAKFAST NEWSLETTER

In one innkeeper's spare time she publishes a newsletter for other innkeepers and guests, and even has a classified section.

HOUSE EXCHANGE DIRECTORIES

Vacationing families find home exchanges more accommodating to the pocketbook. Feeding children in restaurants and putting everyone in hotel rooms is a bit costly but trading homes goes back to the old Roman days with chariots and servants to boot. A monthly directory lists potential house-swappers; who they are, what they have to offer, where, when, and what they have to swap.

INNS

One elegant Englishwoman greets corporate clients at the doorway of her seventeenth-century converted mill and minutes later, having shown them around her home, she goes to the kitchen, dons an apron, and whips up a gourmet meal. Several times a week she provides lunches or dinners to corporate clients in groups of eight to fifty for about $40 a head. When the guests are ready to leave she bids them good-bye sans apron.

Converting your house into an inn is the "in" thing to do. You would certainly be in good company with all the lords and ladies of England who have converted their castles or country manors into hostels for the traveler who wants to live, at least overnight, vicariously. Innkeeping is proliferating in sophisticated cities such as San Francisco and in areas that are off the beaten path. It's a livelihood that can involve the entire family.

Inns ooze charm with special effects: in furnishings, serving high tea to your guests, placing a delectable piece of candy on a turned-down bed cover, cheery fireplaces, continental breakfast. Should the guests leave their shoes outside the door at night, they disappear, only to return before dawn, freshly polished.

An old lighthouse for an inn? Absolutely. Abandoned and functioning lighthouses dot America's coasts; however, few are manned by Coast Guard keepers. No need anymore because of automation. So innkeepers are busy restoring, furnishing, and polishing to provide a safe harbor, dinner, and breakfast for a couple at $125 per night. Leave black tie at home.

Before you succumb to this idyllic calling and invest in an inn, spend time with other innkeepers to see what the business is really like. Read a few inn guidebooks, the bibles of travelers who prefer an inn's unique qualities to a hotel. (See Resources.)

Inns with a past are sometimes referred to as boutique inns. Registered historical sites converted into commercial use supply a good tax break. Under the Tax Reform Act of 1976, restoration costs can be amortized over a five-year period. Because bank financing is not easily available for this kind of enterprise, the tax breaks encourage private investors.

FARMS AND RANCHES

Pitch hay while the sun shines, clean the stables, get up at daybreak? It may be hard for some of my farmer-readers to comprehend why anyone would pay to have the privilege to do the chores, but families do. They want to have that back-to-the-land, hands-on experience with everyman's roots.

In Iowa, there's a rambling, one-hundred-year-old house on a dairy farm where guests are not playing farmhands but hike, and fish, and on Thanksgiving and Christmas hold old-fashioned celebrations featuring sleigh rides and ice-skating.

Oregon has a ranch in Rogue Valley that has excellent meals combined with river-rafting and riding.

Would you mind if someone just wanted to do nothing fancy, just rest, rock a spell on the front porch, and maybe, just maybe, pick some berries.

List your place with one of the companies that specialize in ranchland farm vacations. (See Resources.)

CHILD CARE

Day Care.
Working parents need good quality day care for their children while they are working. The demand exceeds the supply. In most states people who provide these services must be licensed. Kids deserve the best.

Infant Care.
The growing need to provide care for little ones is not being met by presently available community resources. More women than ever before return to work shortly after their child is born and need this service.

Sniffles and Sneezes.
What's a parent to do when the boss expects you and your child has a cold? Communities need more homes like ''Sick Leave,'' were care is provided for sick children.

Drop-In Day Care.
When emergencies arise and there's no one to care for the

children, here's a facility that charges by the hour for child care.

Backyard Play Group.
This is a program for nursery school age children and/or school-age children who need supervision after school hours until their parents return from work.

Respite Care.
Another home service provided for families with handicapped children is called respite care. Weekend foster care gives the parents a breather or respite from a demanding week. Because a handicapped child or adult in the home can place a strain on a marriage, some states pay providers for this service. To keep families intact costs the states less than if the family were on welfare.

Foster Parent.
How do you feel about becoming a foster parent? The Department of Social Service is always in need of good quality homes for young people, infant age through teens, who, for a variety of reasons, require placement outside their own homes. The hard work is rewarding. The number of children placed in a foster care home depends on the size of the house and state regulations. Many single adults can qualify as foster parents.

We were foster parents for a number of years. It wasn't easy to part with the children, but we learned to be happy for them when they were reunited with their families.

Other types of foster care are needed for children and adults handicapped with mental retardation, cerebral palsy, epilepsy, and autism. The fee is higher in these cases, but the amount of care is also more demanding. The social worker provides the necessary support services.

Hotel for Children.
Parents with nonhandicapped children need "alone time," too. Child care that provides a deluxe *special* recreational experience for the children assuages parental guilt caused by leaving the kids behind.

HALFWAY HOUSES

Provide a halfway house for people with or recovering from an emotional illness, or for those experiencing an emotional trauma such as divorce or death of a spouse—people who cannot face the world alone just yet—or post-drug users. Research has demonstrated that institutional care does not work as well as care in small-group family-type community-based homes. Many states are dismantling some of their institutions as these halfway houses are established.

HIDEAWAYS

Nursing care can be given on a short-term or long-term basis in your home. There is a growing demand for recuperative hideaways for postsurgical cosmetic surgery. Face-lifters, coming to a strange city for a special plastic surgeon's skill, do not want or have to go to a hospital, but need a recovery house. They use this kind of facility to hide away for a couple of days or even a week or more at a time. You do not have to be a registered nurse, but you are expected to reassure, pamper, drive, and give assistance as needed. Call your local plastic surgeons and offer your home and services. The monetary reward is quite high.

HISTORICAL TREASURES

Does your house have a historical pedigree? There's rebirth of interest in old-time architecture. Many people are investing in houses of this nature and restoring them to their original character. Nineteen states and five municipalities offer property tax reductions as an incentive to restorers.

If there are a few restored historical houses on your block, a yearly historical walk can become a civic event. That's what the Carroll Avenue residents in Los Angeles do. They show off six houses (with restoration still in progress) to the public each spring, charging $6 per person. In addition to examining the houses, the viewers can buy antiques, photographs, and etchings.

Restoration buffs recommend the resources listed in the

appendix as essential in the search for authentic old-time plumbing fixtures, hardware, etc.

WANNA BE IN PICTURES?

The motion picture and television industries find it less expensive to rent a setting for a location than to build one, as they did in the past. If you feel you have an unusual room, house, driveway, garden, or ranch, send a picture not only to the studios but also to agencies who specialize in media locations. Rentals range from $750 to $5,000 per day. Arrange for an audition.

One owner of a historical house was asked if she didn't find restoration an expensive hobby. She replied that the income from renting her property to film production companies paid for her indulgences. Recently the use of her boudoir in a television commercial allowed her to purchase an antique chandelier.

If you own an office building, boat, plane, or restaurant, these, too, are rentable.

VACATION HOUSES

More and more buyers look at vacation real estate as an investment as well as a recreation retreat. Homes in ski resorts, desert, waterfront properties, spa areas, and mountains have doubled in value in the past two years. Local real estate agents find tenants and keep an eye on the property for fees ranging from 10 to 20 percent of the rent. Don't forget to include boats in this category.

Not only the initial investment but current maintenance expenses of vacation houses can be shared with several families.

During the racing season at England's Ascot, Del Mar in California, or in Saratoga Springs, New York, rents triple or quadruple. Move out of your beach house in the summer, as many people do; get premium rental price for the peak three month season; and return in the fall.

BUY/SELL

What would you think about moving thirty-three times in twenty years? One couple did just that to make a living, buying and selling their home, sometimes completely furnished right down to the filled cookie jar.

Upgrading elderly houses that have gone to seed is a profitable endeavor. One person began by buying a neglected house in a slum area with $3,000 down payment on a $17,000 house. The property was modernized with a bank loan and resold at a considerable profit. With this money the house restorer bought eight more houses, redecorated them in a contemporary style, and sold them. Thirty houses in seven years has made a millionaire out of a slum dweller.

GROUP SHARING

There you are, living in a house that is too lovely to leave, but too large to be practical. Greater numbers of older Americans are choosing to live together, in private homes, helping one another to remain independent. Companionship or assistance in maintaining your home may be just as important as the added income.

DIVIDING THE DWELLING

Call these conversions accessory apartments, single-family conversions, or mother-in-law flats—terms that are cropping up all over the country. The idea behind them is clear: Economics and the scarcity of low-cost rentals are forcing individuals to think of other alternatives.

"Existing single-family homeowners can carve a separate rental-housing unit out of their homes," says Rutgers University's Center for Urban Policy. Over the last five years, about three hundred thousand rental units have been created annually inside single-family homes: apartments within houses, converted basements and attics, duplexes from single family dwellings, and of course, apartments out of garages.

The principal impediment appears to be the zoning ordinances, which in many areas prohibit the conversion of single-family homes. These ordinances vary even within the same city, but most were adopted at a time when America had a higher proportion of traditional family units, a mother, father, and two or three children. These laws are certain to change as owners demand variances to the zoning ordinances. File at your city hall for a variance if you find conversion restriction where you live. Consult your city council representatives so they are familiar with your problem.

The lawmakers in California got the message. Construction of "Granny flats," attached or detached units on the same lots as the older single dwellings, limited to 640 square feet, one or two adults at least sixty years old, are allowed.

Products from A to Z

*The key to survival is having enough
alternatives under one roof.*
— Alexandra Soteriou

ADVERTISING SPECIALTIES

Provide companies with buttons, pens, T-shirts, bumper
stickers, balloons, keychains, calendars with a personalized
advertising message. Whose name is on your pen? How
many companies sent you calendars this year? What is $1\frac{1}{4}$
inches long and $\frac{3}{4}$ inch high and used to be de rigueur to
the sports folk? A little, bitty alligator—worn by the unsus-
pecting public who became walking billboards for General
Mills's subsidiary, David Crystal's Lacoste line. The consumer falls for that kind of status appeal—$450 million
worth of crocodiles. If that trademark is off-limits, there are
others—tigers, penguins, turtles, armadillos, rats, whales.

Buttons, badges, and bumper stickers—say what's on your
mind via the printed word. Slogans, sayings, logos, emblems, identification tags all sell to conventions, organizations, merchants, and individuals. The electronic map
button pin (where the designated city name lights up) is a
natural for the airline industry. Replicas of historical buttons are in for a revival.

Don't forget to advertise your own business and logo with
T-shirts, button pins, bumper stickers, keychains, and any
other means of advertising.

ANTIQUES

Specialize in clocks, duck decoys, toy soldiers, trains, clothing. Building a reputation as a resource for one kind of antique takes a while, but if the collection is of note, customers will come from all over to buy. Specialize in one period of furnishings, or if you can't resist, have some of every period. A compulsive antiques collector turned her home into a small restaurant, using the antiques for atmosphere and profit. Buy and dine.

ART

This list could fill another book, but here's a sampling: soft sculpture, reproductions of famous paintings, portraits, calligraphy, cartoons, lithography, decoupage, decorated porcelain, basketry, picture frames, prints (etchings, woodcuts, linocuts), drawings, computer art, sculptured candles, metal sculpture, Ukrainian decorated eggs, stained glass, origami, watercolors, oils, or replicas of antique jewelry, jars, and pottery, and many more.

Illustrators are much in demand by lawyers for medical drawings as a visual tool of explanation to a judge and jury. For example, if the case centers about injury to a leg, the medical drawings are a pictorial X ray of the anatomy of a leg.

Magazines, books, and brochures also require the services of an illustrator.

A stencil artist changes a ceiling in a home into a wonderland of colorful designs. I grew up in a home whose walls and ceilings were art objects in themselves: some walls were stenciled in a formal rococo design and even on the dining room ceiling bellowy clouds on a pale, blue sky hovered over the spinach.

Batik, an ancient art of putting designs on fabrics with a dye and wax-resistant process, has grown into an exciting business for a couple in Arizona. Their first batik sold for seven dollars at their studio/home/gallery. Now they bring in several thousand dollars each.

One couple made money in "foreign items," from every trip abroad each year. They bought all sorts of decorative clothing, shawls, scarves, gloves, jewelry, ceramics, prints.

When they came home, they made an art gallery out of their living room. The neighbors and their friends were invited in to buy. That's a way of making travel pay for itself.

A neglected form of street art has admirers flipping their lids. Manhole covers are a collector's item. Some of the early covers have art nouveau designs and flowing script. At three hundred pounds you can't hang them over the fireplace, but they can be used for a coffee table base or stepping-stones. Doesn't this prove that just about everything has a value to somebody?

AUDIO- AND VIDEOTAPES

Picture a living room filled with recording equipment, a not too new sofa (that's a compliment) with two old dogs snoozing, and a very pleasant moonlighter seated in front of television screens. He's editing tapes from shows where I appeared, removing the commercials. Many public relations firms hire him to record their clients.

One of his competitors uses a truck as his traveling studio, recording on-the-spot celebrations as well.

Fantasy tapes makes an armchair sports fan into an instant sports hero. Names are dubbed in for any kind of sports event: tennis, baseball, football, soccer, etc. Recorded plays are announced with accompanying sound effects of roaring crowds. This is a great gift item costing between $50 and $100 per tape. (See Video.)

BABY

If you are one of the few who has a beautiful or especially appealing baby, there are films, television, and commercials. And of course, every one of us has that ''special'' kid.

Hand-sewn, crocheted, or knitted baby clothes, quilts, toys, personalized baby gifts, and baby furniture sell well. There's a market in reproductions of ''olde time'' toys. Baby bonnets are now selling in adult sizes!

BALLOONS

Helium-filled balloons with matching six-foot ribbons have replaced the traditional dozen long-stemmed roses as a gift. These ballooneries are springing up all over the country, answering to Balloon Bouquets, Balloon-O-Grams, Hi Flyers, Balloon Boutique. Seems like a no-bust business. Send along a photographer, for an extra fee, of course, to catch the startled ''I don't believe it!'' look of the recipient. (See Greetings under Services.)

BARTER

To swap a cow for grain was familiar to the farmer and now, for city folk, the cow has turned into so many steak dinners in exchange for servicing the restaurant's plumbing. People have rediscovered barter—the cashless economy in which services and goods are traded.

Magazines and newsletters specializing in barter ads are popular. Do you have one in your community?

A Boston barbershop will trade services on the fourth Tuesday of every month. One of its six stylists traded a year's worth of haircuts for services of a divorce attorney. (See Resources.)

BEAUTY PRODUCTS

Look at the popularity of products containing aloe vera, herbs, avocado oil, or seaweed. Health food stores, friends, home beauty parties, and mail order are natural outlets for your famous cucumber mask.

Selling someone else's cosmetics is another of those ''house party'' themes. Several companies offer distributorships; but before you leap, be sure you are enthusiastic about the products. Enthusiasm helps to build sales.

BELTS, BAGS, BUCKLES, AND BRIEFCASES

Buckles have become collectors' items and conversation pieces. In addition to arty handcrafted buckles, there's the commercial kind—companies order buckles with their logo, for employees and customers. Have you seen the cut mirror buckles or the electronic ones that really light up?

I'm a customer of a home artisan who makes her living making and selling belts. From the ceiling of her basement studio hangs a vertical cobweb of different colors of long silk strands, which will be woven into belts of gorgeous, subtle color combinations.

A crafter of leather handbags and briefcases sells his designs at fairs, to a bag manufacturer, and does custom orders, too. He covers all bases.

BIRDS

One person I know specializes in finches, and where does she keep her stock? From ceiling to floor on one living room wall of a one-bedroom apartment.

School for birds? You bet—one man makes his living teaching birds to talk and sing. After graduation the birds are sold.

The record magnate of the bird kingdom operates his business out of his home using subcontractors to help with production. What's on the records and tapes?—''How to Teach Your Bird to Be Multilingual'' and ''How to Teach Your Bird to Sing.'' T-shirts to match are also available.

BREEDER

Here's another long list. There are breeders of dogs, cats, horses, finches, exotic birds, parakeets, fish. There are fifty-six llama breeders in the United States. Buyers use the animals to tote gear, preferring the llama to the mule or horse for western pack trips.

A word of caution and a plea for humaneness! Don't become so greedy that you turn your dog or cat into reproductive factories. Do not breed every time the animal comes into season.

BROOMS AND APRONS

We all know college dropouts, but did you ever know one who is now majoring in brooms and aprons? This dropout has a gallery that specializes in brooms from around the world: upholstered chintzy ones, handwoven, all sizes and shapes, usable or ornamental. The aprons come in all sizes, shapes, and materials, from infants to complete cover-ups for men and women, in fabrics to match kitchen wallpapers. Monogrammed custom aprons are made for restaurants. Extend your lines of merchandise with pot holders, tea cozies, and other kitchen apparel.

BOOKBINDER

Create original bindings and/or restore broken bindings to their former shape. Books on the subject are available at libraries and bookstores. Ask your local art store manager to show you some Italian bookpaper (the old-fashioned inside-cover material with various, often marblelike patterns). If the bookpaper is irresistible, you may be a latent bookbinder.

CABINETMAKER

Given the dimensions by a customer, the actual production of cabinets can take place in a home workshop. Wood turning, too. If you need to brush up on these skills, there are many adult-education classes available; often vocational schools offer good woodworking classes.

CALENDARS

I don't know about your house, but ours is full of calendars. Because I frequently forget which day it is, my husband hung a huge calendar so I couldn't miss seeing the start of each day. But there is money to be made in calendars. A couple of women publish The Master Planner Calendar for their city. It lists all the social and civic events of the year. Does your city have one? Another one I buy is from a nursing home in Massachusetts where the residents publish a calendar with pictures of elderly people. Remember how well the campus calendars sold that featured attractive students? What kind of calendar can you think up?

CAR BUFF

Teach.
University or college extension classes on restoration of antique or classic cars.

Restore.
There's the Corvette lady who makes her living from buying and selling used, reconditioned Corvettes. She rents space to house her stable of twenty Corvettes, although six are parked at her house.

Buy old cars, either assorted makes or specialize in one manufacturer. Restore them yourself or pay someone else to do it and resell them. This is a thriving business.

A friend of mine goes to Europe every year (a business deduction), and there he buys only classic Mercedes, 1964–1968. When they drive off the boat, restoration seems impossible, but when he has finished with them, each car is perfect. I know; I bought one.

Invest.
Will the car you are now driving depreciate or appreciate in value? Owning a car that will be worth more five years from now, like stamps or coins, is considered a business. Few of us think that in relation to the car we drive, whereas we do give consideration to the real estate value of our home five years from now.

On Canvas.
Pay several thousand dollars to see your beloved car on canvas when you haven't gotten around to commissioning a portrait of your spouse and children. Car fanciers do. Posters and greeting cards featuring cars are second best when the cost of a painting is beyond the budget.

CATERER—COOK—CANDY MAKER—BAKER

I love anything to do with the adventure of eating. My stomach is always on the growl. Having served my stint with pots and pans I look to others to turn on my taste buds. Food products provide revenue for many, many homebased businesses. Here are some examples:

Celebrity foods.
The salad dressing and marinara sauce that originated in Paul Newman's kitchen is fighting other established food giants for shelf space in the markets. Another famous television and movie personality—a client of mine—is in the throes of manufacturing a delicious product with the purpose of setting up her daughter in business.

Family recipes make celebrities out of just plain folk, too: Famous Amos, Mrs. Fields, David's, O.G., Miss Grace, Harry and David, Tom and Jerry's.

Food to Send.
A Philadelphia schoolteacher capitalized on the fact that all of us who have moved away from our native cities yearn for hometown foods. For example, there's Philadelphia's hoagies, New York's cheesecake, Cincinnati's pineapple pecan ice cream. New Orleans's poor boy sandwiches, Boston's baked beans. Imagine a mail order business shipping hoagies, that wondrous mix of meat, cheese, tomato, and lettuce, a little olive oil, and oregano on a long, split roll to fifty states and twenty foreign countries. $100,000's worth in 1982. Don't bother making one—it just won't taste as good as Philadelphia's.

Care packages "From Mom" to the "starving" college kids is another mail order business except that "Mom" is a "he" who loves sending packages of goodies to the college crowd from lonesome moms and dads. Some customers place standing monthly orders. Another potential market are care packages to sons and daughters in the armed services.

Caterer.
Not too long ago people only engaged a caterer for very special large events. Not so today. Working couples who want to have a few friends in for dinner or have to entertain

for business reasons, or people like me who have tired of cooking, create a new niche for the food hobbyist turned professional.

They use your kitchen or theirs to do the preparations. If the caterer's house is more attractive than the client's, for a rental charge the party is held in the caterer's home.

Some cooks build their reputation on specialization: ethnic, regional, vegetarian, nouvelle cuisine, barbecue, and others. For example: Middle Eastern fare for private parties and church suppers is a sideline catering business for our CPA.

Nutritious freezer-packed complete meals are delivered to health-conscious customers. Low-sodium or low-cholesterol diets are catered too. No bother anymore to watch one's diet, waistline, or conscience. It's a healthy business for both the owner and the customer.

Love, love, love. Some caterers capitalize on this spiritual food. "Dinner at Eight" will prepare a candlelight romantic repast for two. All provisions made except the ring. And "Breakfast-in-Bed" has a Sunday Special: bagels, lox, and cream cheese, and *The New York Times* delivered to the door.

"Hand to Mouth" works the lunch crowd at beauty shops and offices, offering wonderful salads, thick custom-made sandwiches stuffed with alfalfa sprouts, and fresh fruit drinks from a chilled picnic box. One such vendor is, by her long, layered purple shirts, red-checkered cloth-covered basket perched atop her bandana-wrapped head, a celebrity among her competitors.

You can be the cook and the vendor or package the food and hire others to cover the routes. Many health food stores do not make the sandwiches displayed in their refrigerated cases; they buy them ready-made from vendors.

BAKER

Cakes.
Do you have a cheesecake, fruitcake, or strudel that is a sensational recipe?

One home baker put all six kids through college just on the wedding-cake business. To establish that kind of reputation, baked goods must taste special as well as look pretty.

For some bakers who wish to keep their business in the home, word-of-mouth advertising forces their production to larger quarters. In Los Angeles, "Delights by Dennis," once provided occupational home therapy for a handicapped young man but now has a loyal following at his store. "La Mousse" is another example where success interrupted what was intended as a home operation. Oh, for a slice of pineapple-coconut cake now.

Art Cakes.
Have you ever had your portrait painted in icing on top of your birthday cake? Or had a cake in the shape of a tennis racket or a cello? Edible art usually begins at $75 per cake, depending on the difficulty and time needed to create the masterpiece. If you're a baker and want to get into this, it can be a lucrative homebased business.

Cake-of-the-Month Club.
Desserts made in wonderland: couture cakes, message cookies, keep-forever clay cakes, and other masterpieces are subscribed to just as you would for a monthly magazine.

Entrepreneurial college students arrange for birthday cakes to be sent to fellow students "From Mom and Dad with Love."

Gingerbread Houses.
When we gave the mailman a gingerbread house for Christmas, he said it was the best gift he ever received. Since then we give this old-fashioned state-of-the-art wafer roof shingles, white chocolate bells, gumdrop trees, and red "poinsettias" growing out of marshmallow snowbanks to deserving folk. One couple are taking orders for 1991; they are sold out until then.

Sweet Potato Pies.
This endeavor deserves a special heading because the pies (plus renting rooms in her home) were the beginnings of a millionairess.

CANDY MAKER

When your friends begin to order your special truffles, fudge pecan-caramel corn, or low-cal candies to send as gifts, it's time to take your sweet art seriously. If you are worried about the Health Department's frowning on cooking done in a home kitchen, there are commercial kitchens not used seven days per week. Restaurants, bakeries, church, and temple kitchens can be rented on a part-time basis.

Cheesemaker.
One I know is seventy-four, a Swiss émigré, and for fifty years his homebased business has been a one-man cheese factory. "The Fortuna Cheese Factory" is no secret to those who demand the best Swiss Gruyère and Tilsit. In the factory, the basement of his home, as much as eleven tons of cheese is produced each year.

Jams, Jellies, and Honeys.
The fragrance of hot jams bubbling away in a kettle is nostalgia time. Exotic fruits are in high fashion; kiwi jam is a new, expensive star. One producer turned the garage into a small but mighty assembly-line plant working two shifts to keep up with the demand. Other exotic jam combinations are rhubarb and strawberry, peach and almonds, even chocolate.

Beekeeping can be done in anybody's backyard. Unfiltered, raw honey is coveted by devotees. I send to Mendocino, California, for mine; and on those days that a stronger, more potent nectar is in order, the honey's from Greece. In an enclosed newspaper rack outside a small hotel in Athens, I was amazed to see a beehive, and the hotel owner, a true entrepreneur, sold honey as a sideline. Now that's really productive utilization of space.

One source of information about beekeeping is *The American Agriculturist* (1884). Under "Bee Notes" for April, this magazine cautions the reader to watch for bees showing signs of diarrhea. Apparently, there may be surprising hazards in beekeeping.

Oat Cuisine, Tofu, Kefir, and Yogurt
The big four in the health food movement. Big and little food companies are battling to snare health-conscious con-

sumers. Would you have forecast the fate of oat bran, a nutritious commodity long fed to horses? Just about anything labeled oat bran–enriched, even potato chips dusted with them, is selling to counterbalance high cholesterol levels.

Don't scoff. The homebased corn flake became a hit in 1898; it was touted then as a health food, and now a hundred years later the corn flake is number one in a $5-billion-a-year U.S. dried cereal market.

A New York couple entered the frozen food business substituting low-fat tofu for cheese in lasagne and pizza. This enterprise began when they baked quiches and desserts of tofu from their apartment and sold them at local street fairs. The next move was to a bakery, utilizing the professional facilities when the baker was closed. Greater production allowed sales to health food stores. The story doesn't stop here because a major food company has spread its protective wing over the fledgling producer, thus affording even greater distribution.

CHARTER

Have sailboat, will charter. Boats can be purchased in a lease-back deal. One pair of long-distance operators in Utah finance forty-four-foot yachts and charge $2,000 per week. Since all of the customer contact is by telephone, there is no need to move to the South Pacific where their yachts are waiting for their customers. These two long-distance yachtsmen say that 70 percent per year usage yielded an enchanting $850,000 in 1981.

CHRISTMAS ONLY

Crazy about Christmas cheer? Enough for 365 days a year? Sell only: unusual tree ornaments, fruitcakes, cards, wreaths, gifts, trees. Order real live Santa Clauses here. Orders are placed all year long for Christmas delivery. You don't mind having one part of your house decked out in red, green, and tinsel, to put customers in the mood, do you?

CLOSETEER

The closet manager decorates and organizes closets, including indexing wearing apparel, if you can't remember what you own. With your consent, he or she throws away all the stuff you never had the courage to dispose of. Please come to my house!

CLOTHING

Many homebased businesses successfully concentrate on different aspects of wearing apparel: the unusual, antique, artwear, costumes, used men's, used women's, discount, designer discount, custom-made, uniforms, suits only, sweatshirts and T-shirts, ethnic clothing, and children's wear—to name a few.

Artwear.
Original designs hold particular appeal for many people. For a long time, I have enjoyed collecting art clothing as one would collect paintings. I bought my first tie-dyed velvet shawl at a pre-Christmas show of artisans' crafts held by the local art museum as a fund-raiser. That was it; I was hooked. There's a different aura one feels wearing hand-loved originals.

I have "costumes" (suits) made by a local weaver. Each thread is dyed from the original raw cotton and woven with inspiration. Her clothing causes a sensation everywhere I wear it. Now that she has been "discovered," the prices have soared. And they should have.

How was she "discovered"? In the beginning, she placed the garments on consignment in a few stores. They sold slowly. A woman who had an eye for wearable art asked to be her exclusive sales representative. They agreed. The representative receives 25 percent of the wholesale price. She shows the garments to individuals (in her bedroom) as well as places them in stores. This is an example of how one very talented artisan hit the jackpot and became famous.

Another wearable-art sales representative works on a national scale, discovering clothing artisans from all over the United States. She has the pieces on consignment and puts on shows at museums, exclusive stores, and galleries in all the major cities.

A home designer and manufacturer specializes in hand-painted garments. She designs and sews at home, sells to stores, but twice a year she cleans out her line by holding a home sale for the public.

Women's Ready-to-Wear.

Another true-to-life success story! A husband-and-wife team began their business by designing uniforms for school bands. They branched out into women's fashions, converted the dining room into a workshop with a cutting table, five sewing machines, a pressing board, and a mannequin. Rather than sell to department stores, he opened a small retail store, 12:00 to 5:00 p.m., and sells their designs. They have capitalized on comfortable, easy-to-wear fabrics with minimum detail, one-size-fits-all in dresses; skirts and pants come in small, medium, and large. This home factory has continued for the last fifteen years. The wife's complaint: the neighbors do not consider her a working woman because she's at home—they often send their kids over to her house to play.

Discount.

"Where did you get that stunning outfit?" From California to Maine and from Michigan to Texas the answer is "I-found-the-greatest-discount-place. . . ." Price-conscious consumers are determined in their pursuit of 25 percent to 40 percent off even if it means traveling extra miles. The trend is growing because it's money in the wallet for the consumer. So get going and convert that closet in your bedroom into a discount fashion house. Discount wedding apparel, women's, men's, children's clothing, large sizes, or petites, sport togs, and . . .

Marketing fashion samples and overcuts (merchandise the manufacturer didn't sell) needs only word-of-mouth advertising to build a clientele. It is as pleasurable to tell friends about your find as it is to wear it.

Recycled Men's Clothing.

A San Francisco business deals with really fine men's clothing, discarded for whatever reason, but still in good condition. Men are more secretive about buying used clothing, and a home operation lends more privacy. Files are kept on sizes and styles of regular sellers and buyers.

"Second Hand Rose."
One of my favorite names of used designer garments for women. The garage is full of beautiful clothes, still expensive for the average shopper at secondhand prices, but Rose sells. "Resale," "Second Time Around," "Hand-Me-Downs" are familiar names of these businesses.

Children's Clothing Exchange.
Trade in, trade up, or trade down, the outgrown boys' worn-only-once suits, confirmation dresses, shoes, toys, and furniture.

Tie Tycoon.
One man's necktie homebased business booked sales of $1 million dollars in its fourth year of business. He is the company's only full-time employee, running the business from his house; in fact, a one-man band: designer, bookkeeper, salesman, order-taker, shipping clerk, and telephone operator. He found a niche in the crowded tie market—logo ties. Thirty percent are sales to corporations who want their logos or slogans imprinted. The rest of his business comes from people like you and me who want to send a message via a tie. "Hi Handsome" in backward overall pattern or "S S C" (sexy senior citizen), even "D O M" (dirty old man) sold $60,000's worth one year. Wife, four kids, and his mother help during the Christmas rush.

Another tie manufacturer went into business because she was dissatisfied with tie designs. She did not know how to sew, but knew the fabrics she liked, went out and bought $50 worth of material. She asked her sewing friends to turn out ties from their basement factory. A brown paper bag served as her briefcase to carry the first dozen ties. She called on an exclusive men's store and the buyer thought the ties were stunners and said that the seller's fabric designs filled a void in the store's tie selection. The smart woman is now a tie tycoon. She still uses a contractor to fill orders rather than setting up a factory.

COFFEE SERVICE

Provide the coffee equipment and great coffee to offices on a sale or rental basis. Choose coffee makers that are easy to clean and simple to operate.

COFFIN MAKER

How do you like your coffin? Plain pine or rosewood? Custom-carved with wings of angels? An alternative to the coffin boutiques in mortuaries, which cost on the average $1,000, there is a new homebased casket company that sells coffins for from $75 to $225.

COLLECTIBLES

Autographs, books, coins, Chinese porcelain, primitive American art, Oriental art, jukeboxes, medals, snuffboxes, comic books, antique period furniture, music boxes, folk art, cars, Victorian silver, toys, dolls, old apothecary jars, and games are fun to collect, but if your purpose is to turn a quick buck, try another business. Most times there's a waiting period of three to six months or longer to make a sale. The best bargains come from knowing what you are doing. If you do, you are more likely to unearth that bargain or treasure because the persons selling may not know what they have. (Also see Investments.)

Autographs.
Always have been collectible and a solid negotiable material. But buyers are growing more selective because of a weak economy. George Washington and other founding fathers now sell 20 percent below recent peaks. Film figures have less draw.

Still in much demand are letters of black leaders, famous feminists, and romanticized outlaws. There's a long waiting list for Jesse James letters, which trade at more than $1,000 each. John Lennon's death has created a frantic market for anything with his signature.

Get a letter from Ronald Reagan and you, too, may earn $3,500.

Beer Cans.
Collecting beer cans is easy, inexpensive, and even spawns conventions such as the one held by The Beer Can Collectors of America. The national organization has chapters in major cities. They say it is not unusual for collectors to pay several hundred dollars for an old or rare beer can. Indeed, about seventy-five different cans now command $1,000 or more apiece. The cans in most collections, however, are well within a beer drinker's income, from $1 to $10 per can. That's why collecting has become a national pastime in the last decade.

Did you read about the man who bought a six-pack of Billy beer for $100 and has it stashed away in a bank vault? He heard it has a market value of $6,000.

Miniatures.
The collecting of military miniatures dates to antiquity. Except for dolls, toy soldiers have been the most popular playthings in history. The early sets of metal soldiers by an English toy maker named Britain bring as much as $80 to $2,000.

Paperbacks.
Old paperbacks are the latest form of gold in your attic. Many books with cover prices of 25 cents or even 10 cents, fetch $100 or more. The buyers? Growing ranks of collectors, many of whom chase paperbacks now because market conditions for comic books are tight. Many of the sought-after books are prized for their cover art, especially lurid covers that exploit women. The highest price paid for one thus far is $275. Check your attic!

Button Pins.
A young man received his first Woodrow Wilson button pin as a gift at the age of sixteen. Now at twenty-two, his collection of Woodrow Wilson button pins is worth $35,000. There's an annual convention of button pin collectors, if you're interested. A hot button pin today is the ''Solidarity'' pin from Poland.

Coins and Stamps.
Today few people collect just for the joy of collecting. They want to cash in on their hobby. Not every amateur makes

money. It takes knowledge and patience. Coins normally should be held for several years to show a profit. In numismatics, specialization is said to be the key. Greek and Roman coins, two-cent and three-cent pieces, and trial designs called "Pattern Coins," are a few specialties to consider.

COSMETICS

Products made with jojoba or aloe vera are in vogue. Make your own, or represent a line. Give Avon and Mary Kay cosmetics some competition with the home party method of selling. *The Wall Street Journal* wrote recently that a top cosmetics salesperson averaged about $56,000 annually.

DANCE

Is there a dance doctor in the house? Is your jitterbug out-of-date? Increasing numbers of would-be dancers have discovered a new remedy: a dance doctor who makes house calls at $50 per hour.

DEGREES, SCROLLS, AND AWARDS

Who would like a calligraphy degree from the University of Hard Knocks? One homebased business offers them for $100—yours to frame and show off. This company recognizes that success does not necessarily require an academic degree and that abilities should be applauded.

"World's greatest _____" whatever—grandfather, golfer, loafer—a scroll on antique parchment paper is an alternative to the congratulatory greeting card. Good fun for the customers and recipients and a money-maker for you.

DISABLED

I did not want you to overlook the possibility of offering much-needed services to those who are disabled, so it has a category all its own. One person I know specializes in travel services for the mentally handicapped and persons

113

with hearing or sight impairment. She serves both children and adults, offering both educational and leisure trips. Twenty-four-hour supervision is provided by psychologists, therapists, nurses, and nurses' aides.

DIVORCE

Newly divorced persons are the market for a $15 kit called "Divorce . . . A New Beginning." Included are announcements, party napkins, a booklet of advice, and a souvenir coin with a "Laugh" side and a "Cry" side.

DOG ACCESSORIES

Don't howl at this big business! More than 75 million adorable cats and dogs live in America's households, or 40 percent of U.S. homes are blessed with the pitter-patter of paws. Pet owners live longer. Check University of Pennsylvania's study of ninety-two heart attack patients.

Owners buy his-and-hers mink outfits to match theirs, booties, caps, custom leashes and collars, custom-made dog sweaters and coats, even moccasins for cold climates.

There is personalized dog stationery! And a company that paints a dog's portrait from a photo.

One business offers special doggie diets delivered to the door for dogs who are allergic or are vegetarians.

Does your dog sit up and beg for a bite of your bagel? Share no more. The Bowser Bagel Company brags about their healthy bagels and "old-fashioned goodness."

Did you provide your dog or cat with a Pet Marriage Certificate or a Pick of the Litter Pet Birth announcement? It's a business. Expand the line to include doggie divorce papers, obedience school diplomas, and birthday cards.

Custom dog houses, replicas of your house if that's what you want, provide a living for a carpenter.

DOLLS, DOLLHOUSES, DOLL HOSPITALS, DOLL SHOWS

Dolls.
Welcome to the world of fantasy, where rag dolls become real to their owners. Children? No, adults who spend anywhere from $125 to $1,000 to own a Little Person. It's a highly successful business, $5 million this year, the brainchild of a young artist. To "adopt" a Little Person, prospective owners visit the "adoption center," select a doll, get a birth certificate with the baby's footprints, and one year later a birthday card from Babyland General Hospital. *Doll* is not the only four-letter word to one-hundred thousand proud adoptive parents—another four letter word is *real*!

This is a weird one but it's true. A housewife charges $10 a week to doll-sit while adoptive parents are away. She says, on the average, ten borders are in her playpen each week. I wonder if they miss their folks.

Custom Dolls.
Here's a rather new gimmick, yourself reproduced as a life-size doll, your face, your body build, all of you.

Doll Couturier.
Fashion designs for dolls comprise custom and ready-made costumes and shoes.

Dollhouses.
Have always been loved by everyone. Now adults are making them from kits as a hobby. Make and sell completed dollhouses or kits. They can be museum-bound if they are in the folk art category.

Doll Hospitals.
A rare find today. Do you remember when you poked the doll's eyes out because you were curious about how they worked? And your shrieks and tears of dismay made the family race to the doll hospital for repair. Well, in Georgia, dolls can be taken to the "hospital" and white-coated "doctors" and "nurses" transplant hair, stitch fingers and replace belly buttons. "Vaccinations" with a fabric spray prevent recurrent dirt.

Doll Shows.
"Have collection of fabulous antique dolls. Will chaperon to your store in any city in the United States." So ran an ad from a doll collector. Response was good. A major department store advertised a full-page announcement recently and in part, it read: ". . . Sit in on seminars given by these renowned doll creators and collectors and view their private collection."

ELECTRIC POWER

The Mom and Pop Power Co. provides electricity from a small power plant for six hundred homes. Tapping power from a creek that cascades down a mountain in the couple's backyard provides $40,000 to $60,000 each year for a $150,000 investment. A high-powered way to use up their six kids' energy was to teach them all to be powerhouse operators. The story of this family affair should encourage others to form small power companies.

ENTERTAINMENT

Rent yourself out for parties, as a clown, puppeteer, magician, or Punch and Judy. You'll need a costume and routine to work as a clown. The other party characters and activities listed here require specific skills and abilities.

EXERCISE

Workouts on wheels now bring exercise to where the flab is. Many well-heeled people have decided that working out in gyms is déclassé. They now can order a mobile health club: customized van, which is lit, carpeted, air-conditioned, and fitted with a complete set of weight equipment, an exercise bike, and a rowing machine. Or if you just want someone to work out with you sans van, call a trainer who will run, swim, play tennis, or teach aerobics. About $50 per hour.

FARMING

I get so many letters from people who live in rural areas in need of supplemental income. "What can we do?" they ask. Let me offer a few suggestions.

Specialization, such as raising organic vegetables and fruits is a winner because the supply does not meet the demand. The public is on alert. Visit a health food store featuring organic produce to be convinced by the number of customers.

Capitalize on specialty products associated with your region. When I think of Vermont, maple syrup comes to mind. And what do I buy? Maple syrup from Vermont, of course. Regional specialties work well for a mail order business. Recently I received a small booklet from a homebased firm in Oregon featuring "regionally unique gifts and gourmet foods." Red Chinook salmon, albacore tuna, filberts, and whale mugs are some of the items.

Many city people like to give themselves and their children a farm experience. Can you turn a spare room into a guest room and let your paying visitors join in with the farm chores? List your accommodations with the bed and breakfast associations.

Handmade products produced by individual farmwomen is another way to earn money. Here are examples of small businesses that are growing in popularity with public demand: quilts, wooden and fabric home decorations, food products, leather chaps and saddles, jogging suits for city people, dolls and doll clothes. Begin by selling at fairs and craft shows. When you can't keep up with the demand, hire your neighbors.

Front and Backyard Farming.

Many years ago, I was determined to produce my own fresh eggs in the backyard. My knowledge about chickens was meager, and the business never hatched. However, with the rage for range-fed chickens today and the supply too small, you may want to consider this.

True, sizes of available outside space differ, but you will be surprised what small plots of ground can produce in cash. Specialist farmers get rich in their own backyards. One man's small backyard is crammed with exotic basils and thymes in wide rows, pots of chervil under a screen, rosemary bushes,

Italian parsley—all the herbal delights prized by chefs. He says, "Two people really working at it can easily earn $1500 to $2000 a week because there is no overhead."

My neighbor planted all varieties of cacti in his hilly front yard, and that's his mail order product! A famous movie and television star dug up his front yard, and put in an organic vegetable garden. Granted, *he's* not doing it for extra income; but *you* can.

Are you familiar with the biodynamic/French intensive gardening method used on minifarms? A 20 × 5 foot lot could raise 322 pounds of vegetables and soft fruits, averaging out to a return of $6 to $7 per hour for time spent if the retail price is used to calculate its value.

A 100 × 100 foot plot, planted in the ordinary way is supposed to yield about $800 worth of vegetables. Do you remember how good a tomato can taste? Homegrown tomatoes will have customers knocking at your door, or they can stop at your roadside stand.

Cash in on trendy food fads. For example, if your climate permits, grow the unusual: edible flowers used in cooking or as decoration in restaurants are much in fashion. Or baby vegetables—watercress, arugula, mache, red romaine, and other varieties of tender greens—provide a living for a backyard tenant farmer. Near Santa Barbara there's a two thousand-tree banana farm on just four acres—a first with forty varieties.

Escargot.
Escargot from a backyard snail? Yes, there are a few entrepreneurs who catch them, using a feeding technique to clean them out, and are marketing the all-American snail (formerly from France).

Weeds.
Perhaps you would rather let your yard turn into weeds. One couple can brag about theirs. Lovely dried arrangements of rabbit tobacco and pepper grass, preserved with hair spray, earns them a full-time living.

Aromatic Herbs.
In Norfolk, England, what was once a small lavender farm is now a big homebased enterprise. There's the cut lavender, the oil to sell, their own fragrance, sachets, guided

tours (admission fee), soaps, talcum, bath gel, scented papers, and to top off all your purchases, scones and tea in the cottage garden. The point of their success to remember is how many ways the clever owners generate cash.

Avocados.
Seven years ago, as a moonlighting endeavor, a college student planted twelve acres of avocados. Last year the grove yielded 117,000 pounds of avocados.

Christmas Trees.
Crops that take a few years to mature, such as Christmas trees, can provide a tidy sum for retirement.

FISH FARMS.

Aquaculture.
Mass-produced fish, in processing plants with controlled water environments, will be the wave of the future. Catfish ponds, frogs, crawfish, salmon, trout, red snapper, shrimp, lobster, koi, oysters, and abalone are being farmed now. It does not require a big spread; a couple of acres could house a fish farm.

Other things to grow for profit include earthworms, rabbits, squabs, pheasants, ladybugs, minks, kiwis, pine nuts, pistachios, citrus, kumquats, ginseng, truffles, and praying mantises.

FIREWOOD

Selling firewood can provide a supplementary income for you. It works well for a working couple I know of, producing extra income and vigorous exercise—they split logs. In their woodsy neighborhood, people are always pruning and trimming trees. The couple pick up the trimmings, let them dry in their backyard, use the smaller pieces in their own fireplace, and save the choicer chunks to sell for $20 per truckload (about three-fourths of a cord). That is a bargain for their customers. They work on their woodpile only when they feel like it and are proud of adding about $400 to their income each year. Children can help carry, unload, and stack the wood. A few splinters will start them on their way to entrepreneurship.

FLOWERS

They do not have to be real to be picked as a business venture. Silk, porcelain, and paper have their own following.

U.S.-grown pussy willow branches bring $7.50 per branch wholesale. At the market they sell three twelve-inch sprigs for $3.50. One crop a year can realize a couple of hundred in extra money. If the climate is right, plant gardenias and sell direct to the local florist. A potted stephanotis will produce large sprays of white, waxy, fragrant flowers, used in wedding bouquets. Price those at your florist, and you will treat that treasure with great respect and pride. Violets, exotic peonies, lilacs, or lilies of the valley have appeal.

Specialize in the unusual flowers; more than fifty varieties are in fashion. Florists enjoy new business growth with the exotic. Americans are buying flowers in greater abundance, and demand for the unusual varieties is growing. There's a new, more discriminating clientele. Although the fresh-cut flower business rose 29 percent between 1979 and 1980 to 2.7 billion (according to *Floral Report*, a trade publication) attracting franchisers and conglomerates, the business is still largely composed of individual entrepreneurs. Even in a depressed economy, people use flowers as a pick-me-up. They are recession-proof.

Although the agricultural department reports that roses and carnations were last year's best-sellers, rarer blooms are moving up fast, particularly in urban areas. Bouquets of monkey paws, apple blossoms, dutch onion flowers, and ginger flowers arrive by jet daily.

FURNITURE DESIGNER

Freelance contract with manufacturer is the way one designer/manufacturer works. With a homebased drawing board and a contractor who makes the furniture, the designer is able to market it under her label.

GAMES

You'll be the winner if you have an idea for a new game. There's the choice of selling the game to one of the major game producers or becoming your own company.

If you sell your game to another company, there's the option of an outright sale with you retaining no rights or cash up front plus royalties. Since the average successful game sells about one million copies a year, royalties would be my choice. See *your* attorney for advice.

Others choose to become their own assembly line with family members helping out and marketing their game. One such family venture is a series of children's ecological board games honoring Mother Nature. The games are sold at fairs, through mail order, and publicized by ads and reviews in magazines and newsletters concerned with teaching about nature.

To save production costs, another designer/market-researcher/producer/promoter is so convinced his board game will hit the jackpot that he mortgaged his home. The first five thousand games, assembled by good wife and relatives in the den of his home, are now on the market. He says "the idea for a product is 5 percent of its success, and marketing constitutes the other 95 percent."

P.S. Trivial Pursuit, originally a homebased effort, set the record in sales in 1984 when 20 million games were sold. And Pictionary, another home-hatched concept, sold 350,000 in 1986 but hit its stride with 3 million in 1987.

GARAGE SALES

It's one matter to have an outlet for the yearly discards from spring cleaning yet another to make one's living from week-end garage sales. People do. In front of apartment buildings, street corners, homes you can see clothes, furniture, toys, and other stuff. Makes me wonder sometimes if there's anything left in their homes.

Experienced garage salespeople offer their services to individuals who have merchandise but don't want to mess with putting on their own show. The "professional" gets a percentage of the receipts.

GARDEN STANDS
DOOR-TO-DOOR—STREET CORNERS

Even a small garden stand can contribute toward the rent. If you live on a busy street corner where cars have to stop, it is an ideal location for a flower, plant, or vegetable stand. The merchandise can be from your own garden or purchased at the wholesale markets.

In Los Angeles just about every busy intersection has vendors selling bags of oranges or bouquets of carnations. Many of us buy whether we need oranges or not, just to encourage the industrious.

Door-to-door selling has made an amazing return. Neighborhood people wait to buy their produce from vans that have a regular schedule. Some vendors specialize in ethnic neighborhoods, knowledgeable of the kinds of popular fruits, vegetables, and spices their customers will buy.

One of the most ingenious offices I've ever seen is located at a corner vegetable and fruit stand. The public telephone booth nearby serves as the office phone, with crates piled around it to prevent public access. Now, that's chutzpah!

GIFT BASKETEER

"A tisket, a tasket, a green and yellow basket"—Remember that song and when it was the custom to welcome a new neighbor with a basket of your homemade goodies or send one over to an ailing friend? Today baskets of various sizes and themes are rivaling floral bouquets in popularity. Baskets are filled with assorted foodstuffs, some that demand an immediate picnic or others with such items as toys, or cosmetics, or filled with a variety of plants. Use your imagination; decorate lavishly with originality.

GREETING CARDS

Fifty-five million greeting cards were sold in 1980 by a young, talented woman working from home without a staff. This artist is under contract with a company to produce a specified number of cards each year and is one of the few greeting card artists to receive a royalty (terms set by her) rather than selling the designs outright. According to the National Association of Greeting Card Publishers, about seven billion cards are sold each year—half of all the personal mail sent in this country!

HERBALIST

There's been a rebirth of interest by the general public in the use of herbs medicinally. Some cultures always have used herbs as curatives and preventatives for external and internal disorders. Just look at the phenomenal sales in herbal teas—consumers quarrel about the merits of rose hips, chamomile, peppermint, ginseng, hibiscus flowers, lemon grass, orange blossoms, eucalyptus. There are herbalists who specialize in mixing brews for the treatment of ailing four-legged animals. The medicine man returneth.

HOME PARTIES

Think of how many kinds of home parties you have been to—Tupperware, discount clothing, cosmetics, silverware, jewelry, perfume, art, cleaning products, vitamins, herbs, children's toys, adult toys, sexy lingerie, vitamins, and herbal soaps and toiletries. Home parties can be planned and given in areas that are conveniently located for you. If you enjoy socializing and meeting people, this can be a pleasant activity as well as a profitable one.

Be careful to investigate thoroughly before you invest in one of those costly sample kits. Some companies make their money just by selling the kits to eager customers who can't wait to get started. It doesn't take too much more cash *to develop your own line*. Buy one of a kind for the original display to market-test the products before buying by the dozen.

HOROSCOPES

''Dial-A-Horoscope'' operates with no cost to the caller. Then, who pays? Local businesses purchase a twenty-five-second telephone commercial that precedes the horoscope forecast. The operators of this inspiration from the stars never go near the phones. It is all done with a computer program.

IMPORTER

There is much activity in the importation of ethnic products from other countries. Chinese goods are very popular now. For home galleries, specialize in Alaskan art, jewelry, Japanese boxes, Guatemalan dresses, or folk art from some other places. Find an unusual item, something not seen in every department store. Try to get the exclusive right of distribution. Sell for less than the stores or the museum gift shops. A wonderful fringe benefit is the tax-deductible travel expenses incurred in the line of duty. (See Resources section in the back of the book.)

INSECTARY

Moths (yes, moths), ladybugs, praying mantises, caterpillars, and other friends are homegrown for organic gardeners and schools. I once ordered ten thousand assorted ladybugs and praying mantises to control the aphids; then released in the dark evening per instructions, I awoke the next morning to discover the newcomers preferred the roses next door.

INVENTOR

It's the American dream—to invent something and get rich from it.

Don't think you have to compete with an Edison or an Alexander Graham Bell in order to make the world take notice of your inventions. The person who invented the bobby pin did very well indeed. Push a series of buttons in an Oregon home and the house gets cleaned, laundry washed and dried, dogs and cats bathed. While all these suds are flowing, the sixty-seven-year-old, liberated inventor is continuing to build (by herself) this self-cleaning house.

Two television actors were watching daytime soap operas when Zow!, they got an inspiration—not from the soap opera story, but from the commercials for laundry detergent, dish-washing liquid, and similar products. The result is "Day-time Soap," a fragrant bar of soap packaged in a box resembling a television set.

Any original idea for a service or a product is an invention. Getting the idea and doing something about it is what this book is about.

One invention recently marketed is a phone booth that provides credibility. Called "What's Your Excuse?" it is a custom-built pay telephone booth that has fourteen different background-noise tapes—sounds to enhance whatever tall story the caller is giving to boss, wife, friend, or creditor. Background sounds include bullets whining, airplane noises, jailhouse noises, and others. The inventor sells Excuse Booths to bars. The trick is staying sober enough to push the right button to match your excuse. (See section on Protection.)

INVESTMENTS

There are other kinds of investments besides art, gold, silver, Persian rugs, stocks, bonds, real estate, cattle. Baseball trading cards that sell to collectors from $1.00 to $25,000. Half a million serious card collectors in the United States are dealing. A Buck Rogers water pistol originally sold in 1932 for 39 cents—today it is valued at $100. A Mickey Mouse watch in the original box sold in 1932 for $2.50—today it's worth about $300. Old comic books bring bucks. Which products that we use today will be cherished collectors' items fifty years from now? (Also see Collectibles.)

JUNKYARD

Remember when discards were in disrespect? They're not anymore. "Recycling," using a salvaged piece in a new way, is the thing to do. Confessionals from demolished churches become restaurant phone booths, pulpits are used by maître d's to hold their reservation book, stained glass windows from a Victorian house are purchased for a new structure. Demolishing is past tense; restoration-conscious consumers love gingerbread trim, wrought iron gates, gargoyles, old paving, and brick. Nostalgia is in. DON'T throw it out; it's valuable.

LAMPSHADES, WASTEBASKETS, TISSUE HOLDERS

Handpaint any of these items or cover them with fabric that matches the wallpaper. Handsew custom lampshades in antique or modern reproductions.

LEATHER GOODS

Belts, purses, sandals, custom shoes, book covers, wallets, leashes, dog collars, attaché cases, and time management organizers are all popular leather items to make and market, wholesale and/or retail. . . .

LOVE LETTERS

This service provides the words to fit the occasion and the blank page. You can select any one of twenty-five stock letters for anniversaries, birthdays, apologies, and so on or request a custom message that expresses your thoughts. About $12 for stock and $25 for custom.

LOVELESS MESSAGES

Dead flowers with an attached card "You'll get yours," signed "Unsigned" from Drop Dead Flowers. The owner calls the service "an elegant alternative to a pie in the face." He says his flowers have gone, usually anonymously, to "former lovers, parents, business associates, ex-friends."

MAILBOXES

We know that the price of stamps continues to increase but $5000 and up for a mailbox? The price of a one-of-a-kind art piece designed with your personality in mind. Ah, what the rich will do with their pennies.

MARRIAGE MARKETING

Here's a woman who created an international matchmaking business, working from her home. Her fame spread to Asian women who are looking for American husbands. She, herself, came to the United States as a mail order bride, so she knows her business. She compiles a catalog from the applicants and sends it for a fee to thousands of men all over the world.

Another idea that is catching on in several cities is the bachelor book *A Woman's Guide to Single Men in* . . . (name of city). The book lists biographies, photos, names, and addresses of men from twenty-two to sixty. One such book tells women what to say in letters, what stationery to use, and how to close a letter. The men are found through friends and ads and charged $150 for the privilege of being listed. How about doing a bachelor (either male or female) directory for your city? Certainly offers an alternative to the singles bar.

MESSENGER SERVICE

Individuals, law offices, and publishers use messengers to pick up things and deliver, take packages from one part of town to another. So do many other businesses.

MINIATURES: ALIVE AND OTHER KINDS

What stands fifteen inches tall, eats strawberry Jell-O for breakfast, has a potbelly, curls up on his mistress's lap to watch the evening news? An adorable mini-pig.

If you want to raise livestock in your backyard, here's how: breed miniatures. Pint-size animals are a very big hit with pet lovers. Horses, pigs, donkeys, rabbits, and even goats are the current craze. Pedigreed or not, each has its own association, from ten thousand pygmy goat owners to twenty-eight thousand miniature horse fanciers.

The interest in miniature animals dates back hundreds of years, as well as the fascination for collecting other kinds of little stuff, such as cups and saucers, dollhouse furniture, dolls, animal figures, and so on. Anything small can develop into something big for the collector.

MUSIC

There's a market for old-time player pianos, nickelodeons, harpsichords, antique music, piano rolls. Converting pianos to player pianos, making custom-made guitars, violins, banjos, harpsichords, and pianos finds many customers.

A hurdy-gurdy maker says business is hunky-dory because he has advance orders to keep busy for one and a half years.

A famed musician has built a recording studio in his backyard for his own use and also rents to others.

NEEDLE ART

Naturals for home business are embroidery, monograms, quilts, knitted and crocheted garments, and needlepoint. Dresses and sweaters, in particular, are in vogue, as well as crocheted ski caps. Also popular are stuffed animals, dust ruffles, old-fashioned Jean Harlow satin pillows, and bedspreads. On my last plane trip to Europe I commented to my traveling companion that the number of stuffed animals carried aboard by children and adults alike made me wonder if there would be enough room for all of us.

ORAL HISTORIAN

This service records the family's accounts of happenings and events and puts it all together on a tape for posterity. Provide an accompanying film of family pictures from the past to the present generation.

ORTHOTICS

A properly trained, credentialed orthodist can make custom supports, arch supports, back supports, shoulder braces, and so forth, by doctors' prescriptions. One such orthodist uses his garage as a laboratory, heeding safety codes (there are two fire extinguishers, one for chemical/electrical, and one for combustibles). The fittings for the patients can take place in the doctors' offices or in hospitals.

PAPER BAGS

The lowly yet indispensable brown paper bag has come into its own. An artist has built a homebased business using the grocery bag to make custom-made party decorations, greeting cards, and gifts. If the paper bag was good enough for Picasso to use in his early collages, then it's time for it to claim its fame.

PUBLISHER

''You don't make much money on a weekly with a circulation of 550 but I wouldn't trade my life with anyone,'' insists the sixty-eight-year old woman, editor and publisher, copywriter, photographer, ad taker of the *Imperial Valley Weekly* for thirty-one years. No small accomplishment in itself but add sole breadwinner to seven children by publishing the paper and that's really an accomplishment.

Gazettes, newspapers, reviews, catalogs, books, trade journals, magazines, periodicals, newsletters are some of the kinds of printed matter published and sold today. Self-publishing can be profitable. If your book or books sell, the profit to you as self-publisher can be greater than the 6 to 15 percent of the sales that would come to you through established publishing houses. Really bone up on all facets of book production and marketing *beforehand* if you decide to be your own publisher. One author of legal textbooks self-published so many of his own works that he opened a book manufacturing company, too.

Rejection slips authors receive may not be an accurate indicator of the marketability of their manuscripts. Take the following example.

How could a fourth-generation Oregon man write a guidebook for Manhattan? An outsider! New York publishers would not consider the idea and oh, are they eating their copies of rejection letters! The author put up his own money to publish ten thousand copies and anticipated sales of two thousand or three thousand. Instead, he sold seventeen thousand—through the mail, through New York bookstores, hotels, gift shops, and even a delicatessen.

What does this prove? That experts can be quite wrong. So don't be intimidated. Believe and proceed. The Oregon author is working on his third edition of this book, rejecting with glee the offers to take over publication and distribution by the New York publishers.

Catalogs.

Many mail-order entrepreneurs broaden their line of merchandising via catalogs. According to the Direct Mail/Marketing Association, there are about eight thousand catalog mail-order companies specializing and focusing on narrow audiences, as magazines or newsletters do. About forty catalogs are received by residents yearly.

A successful catalog sales outfit that specializes in business-attire maternity clothes was conceived by a twenty-nine-year-old mother who got the idea when she became pregnant. At the time she was working at an office and had to buy businesslike clothing two sizes too big in order to maintain a professional look. Maternity clothes styles are most times overly decorative and frilly. When the wives' homebased businesses begin to have that sweet smell of success, husbands quit their jobs, as in this case. He is now vice-president of marketing and her father assists. Another example of squeezing into a market that would seem overcrowded but there was a need that was not being met.

Small Book Publishing Industry.

Can it still be called a "cottage industry" when cities can get an identity and build on it for jobs and prestige? Santa Barbara, California, is to the book publishing industry what Santa Fe, New Mexico, is to artists. Santa Barbara has attracted 10 percent of all the small publishers in the United States. One hundred twenty-two book and forty-one periodical publishers provide four thousand jobs, five hundred in two- and three-person staffs, and an estimated 3,500 jobs in the allied field of design, typesetting, printing, advertising, distributing, and writing.

Warning: On returning home one day, a fellow publisher discovered all the cartons of stored books in the attic had crashed through the ceiling down into the living and dining rooms. Remember that tomes weigh a ton.

Newsletters.
If you can find a subject that is not already covered by the one hundred thousand plus newsletters, this is the business for you. Ninety-five thousand of them are organization and company vehicles, so that leaves a competitive force of five thousand. These are consumer-oriented: collecting (whatever), travel, crafts, cooking, money, technical, business opportunities, health, advocacy, politics, and so on.

My favorite is *Chocolate News*, a bimonthly, milk chocolate-colored paper with dark chocolate print, and it even smells of (not-the-best) chocolate. Unfortunately, the publisher sends only chocolate beans, recipes, confectionary news from here and abroad, nary a piece of candy. By page three, the craving is too great, and off to the nearest Hershey for a quick fix!

To further illustrate how newsletters can appeal to subscribers with esoteric tastes: here's a sampling:

Garlic. Have you read *Garlic Times* lately?

Llamas. For all you llama fans, there are two newsletters on llamas. Sorry, they are not dailies. Get both; you might miss something. If you don't know where to write, attend the National Llama Convention in Bend, Oregon, in July.

Bargains. *Best Bargains* newsletter offers the best sources in the city in clothing, restaurants, movie houses, and so on. Could your city use a newsletter like this?

Cars. Own a Rolls-Royce? Recently I was corrected when I referred to the car as a "Rolls." It's called a "Royce" by the "in" group and has its own "in" newsletter, with the subscribers' incomes averaging more than $200,000. This opens up endless possibilities for all the other brandmakes that are traveling around without their own newsletter.

Refunds. Sixty-some newsletters cater to refunders. As prices continue rising, more and more shoppers are swapping and trading information in what has become a nationwide network of refunders.

Neighborhood. Beverly Hills, California, has its own newsletter, mentioning names, places, and events related only to Beverly Hills. Advertisers subsidize its publication and it is free to residents. Who doesn't like to read about themselves? It's a money-maker.

NOTE: The experienced publishers say it is not difficult to get the first subscribers; its the renewals that measure success.

QUILTS

Shoppers are responding to products that are handmade. Quilts are in this category, thus their high sales merit a separate listing here. They are sold at exclusive shops from Fifth Avenue to Rodeo Drive, at fairs, and in art museums.

Remember when Appalachia's homebased mountain women had a corner on the quilting market and for $10 one of their beauties was yours? Today quilts range from $200 to $1,000 or more.

RECIPES

Advertised in the classified ad section of many magazines are the specialty recipes of individuals around the country. "Send $2.00 for Ma's best-ever cheesecake recipe." And people do. Figure it out—classified advertising costs relatively little, photocopied recipes, about three cents each, envelope, and stamp, and you've got a business.

SECURITY SYSTEMS

With the crime rate at an all-time high, people are trying to put the Great Wall of China around themselves and their homes. From police whistles to elaborate antiburglar home devices, protection aids are a thriving business. Just look at the number of mailers you receive soliciting business. Got another foil-proof idea?

Watch Ducks.
Yes, rentable ducks are live, first-line-of-defense protectors. Ducks quack and gabble plenty when an interloper appears.

Signs of Security.
Can you stencil signs? There is great demand for signs such as "Guard Dogs on Duty," "Beware of Owner," "There's Nothing Left—We Were Robbed Last Week," and the like.

Human-size dolls are being sold to serve as silent companions. They drive with their owners late at night in the car or they create a silhouette against a drawn drapery or shade. Can you sew a convincing cloth figure or design a life-size inflatable figure? There's a market for them.

Patrol.
Start your own patrol company.

SOUVENIRS

Providing souvenir items can be homebased business that involves selling souvenirs made by others or making and selling them yourself.

People seem to want mememtos of both public and private events. Just think of all the wedding matches you've collected and hesitate to put to practical use out of respect for sentimentality.

England balanced the budget with all the commemorative items before and after THE wedding.

Souvenir items include coins, postcards, T-shirts, ashtrays, drinking mugs, volcanic ash, canned smog, and on into infinity. If you wish to use someone's trademark or registered logo, art, design, or cartoon characters, you must get permission. Did you know it costs a fortune to obtain just the okay from Disney Enterprises to use any of their registered designs?

SPECIAL EVENTS

You can cash in on the special events held in your city or state such as conventions, political events, commemorative occasions. For example, for the Olympics in Los Angeles or the World's Fair in New Orleans housing shortages are expected. Rooms, apartments, or houses for rent are commodities many people have. What other services do visitors need?

What kind of commemorative gidget can you create? One election year we shipped red, white, and blue donkeys and elephants to you know who.

SPERM DONOR

Sperm banks pay for each acceptable ejaculation from a healthy, intelligent male whose name is withheld from the matched infertile couple. Reproduction takes place without sex through artificial insemination.

STATIONERY

Perhaps you would enjoy custom-designing letterheads, calling cards, invitations, and announcements for every occasion. You work with clients directly, using original designs or stationers' catalogs. A class in typography and/or basic design, graphics design, and commercial art would be helpful to you.

STONECUTTER

Making a living out of chiseling epitaphs into gravestones and making monuments and grave markers is a $700 million-a-year industry nationwide. About as close to a recession-proof business as one can find.

TELEPHONE SERVICES

Sales.
Even banks are now using "cold calling" to sell their customers IRA or Keogh plans. Many other kinds of companies use telephone sales to line up prospects or to sell directly to the consumer. Carpet cleaning, home improvements, insurance, encyclopedias, storm doors and windows, magazine and newspaper subscriptions, fund-raising, cemetery lots

(euphemistically and gravely called "pre-need plans") are only a few who use the phone as a hotline to generate sales.

A major office supply company whose receipts are in the millions uses only the telephone to sell their products. Their sales force of twelve makes 130 calls per day, offering low, low prices.

Many new telephone solicitors either hate the pressure and frequent rejection of the job or they thrive on it. It is common for a homebased business to use the phone for promotion because phone work is low-cost advertising.

Wake-Up Service.
For those heavy sleepers who ignore the wafts of aromatic coffee and the sounds of clock radios, provide a homebased telephone wake-up service.

Slow Payers.
The medical profession and businesses sometimes hire outside services to remind customers via the telephone about past-due bills. This is a natural for homebases.

Answering Service.
If good service is offered, prepare to be swamped with clients. The growth of the mechanical answering device is largely because of the unavailability of skilled telephone message service operators.

Hotlines.
Some examples are:

Drug—From his garage a pharmacologist has operated a drug hotline for consumers concerned with conflicting effects of the drugs they are taking. Hospital-funded.

Stocks—To receive information about stock market facts costs fifty cents. Two thousand callers daily.

Anagrams.
One entrepreneur tied up five hundred telephone numbers in the hope that companies will want access to one of his numbers as part of their marketing strategy. (Refer to section on Promotion.) Remembering a phone number that describes the business is easy to recall.

135

Tape Recordings for People's Answering Machines.
Surely you have heard "Hello" in Donald Duck, Humphrey Bogart, or Mae West. Who buys them? People who want to squeeze some fun out of the telephone or those who get stage fright in recording their own voices.

Custom Phone Service.
Expert will analyze the client's phone traffic and furnish equipment and installation.

TOY LIBRARY

A Vermont couple will share their one thousand toys but for profit. Seesaws, games, piano, and computers are included in the lendable items. Members pay $60 a year to borrow for three weeks at a time. Also used by some local school systems.

TRADE-IN PRESENTS

Wedding gifts that cannot be returned are brought in for appraisal and then traded down or up on something else. You need not specialize in just wedding presents. Any-occasion presents can be exchanged. Absolute discretion must be guaranteed. Mum's the word.

UNDERWEAR

When is underwear *lingerie*? At home parties and certainly when husbands buy it for their wives, it is. And that is what husbands are doing—at very sophisticated salons where buxom models deliver a sales pitch wearing sheer merchandise. The models socialize, accept a drink or two, but only the nightie is for sale. The brains behind this enterprise is a highly successful gray-haired grandma who plans to franchise and expects to become queen of the lingerie trade.

VIDEO

Programming, production, distribution, just about anything to do with television, particularly in cable television, is a major growth industry.

Video Fashion.
Too busy to go to Paris to see the spring collection? All the European haute couture is on tape, if you'd like a home showing. Many local women's clubs like to have private showings as fund-raisers. It could raise your own funds substantially.

Video Inventory Service.
A method of documenting a homeowner's or businessperson's possessions. The owner shows and describes each item on a color cassette, receives the finished tape to keep in a safe deposit box.

Video Wills.
The client writes his/her will and appears on film telling posterity how to dispose of the estate. It is shown after death on a bigger-than-life screen. Unfortunately, it's a short run, but profitable for heirs. Oh, well, that's Hollywood.

Video Love Letters.
Make videotapes for your clients who can't say "I love you" face-to-face. Romance-on-tape is the answer. For people who can't say "I don't love you" in person, use tape to wind down the affair.

VINEYARDS

Here's where the grapevines can pay the bills for a serious vintner or provide an extra income for the hobbyist. And think of the fringe benefits. The wine industry has discovered that grapes can be grown in so many more regions throughout the United States than just Napa Valley.

The thought of owning a vineyard conjures up all kinds of romantic dreams: châteaus, tastings, trips to France, and tax write-offs. But remember, growing grapes is farming, and farming is hard work. Success is subject to nature's whims and a strong back. What small vintners bottle in a year, the giant wineries fill and cork in an hour. Nevertheless, a toast is in order—"to the success of your homebased business."

WHOLESALE CATALOGS

This business requires not stock, just an assortment of catalogs from which the customer chooses furniture, jewelry, clothes, or appliances. The merchandise can be delivered directly to the consumer from the factory.

WIGS

One woman has built a business catering to style-conscious women who can't give up wigs. In observance of Hebraic law, which forbids a married woman to let anyone but her husband see her hair, many orthodox Jewish women wear wigs, but still want to be fashionable. Beginning a business at fifteen years of age styling wigs, one entrepreneur sells twenty-five thousand wigs a year. Wholesale and retail sales are about $850,000. Women pay her $200 to style a wig.

Don't keep this one under your hat. Wigs are worn by many people for fashion purposes and (sadly) because of hair loss resulting from chemotherapy.

WILD WEST

Custom Western outfits, bonnets and boots, and square dance frocks for the city folk.

Hire-a-Rodeo.
Now here's a company that will put some of that old West spirit into a backyard party. Comes complete with barbecue, square dance fiddlers, caller, and teacher of the dance steps for the guests.

WINE

Personalized Labeling.
Not only can the wine be purchased at discount but the client's name will be printed on the label.

Tours.
A conducted tour of the wine country comes with a lavish picnic lunch, a hot air balloon ride over the grapes, and many sips.

WOOD CARVING

A hobby that fits the bill is carving pelicans and game birds. Hand-carved duck decoys, knives, letter openers, totem poles, sculptures—all have buyers. Also, you can teach this art to others.

WRITING

Pen Pal Letters.
"Letters for little people from Uncle George—a different gift for children aged three to seven" . . . That's the way the ad reads. With a little advertising, you may find many other markets for letter-writing service.

Copy.
Advertising copy can be done on a freelance basis for all kinds of media.

Verse.
Long or short rhymes for holidays, special events, birthdays, bereavements can be submitted for acceptance to greeting-card companies. Better yet, start your own company.

Articles.
Got an angle? One freelance writer sold different versions of an article on homebased businesses to eight different magazines and newspapers.

Books.
True confessions, articles, westerns, mysteries, cookbooks. Romance novels are really "in." Fifteen million fans consume thirty to forty books every month. An author, turning out four or five sixty thousand words of love each year can earn about $50,000.

Scripts.
Television, movies, plays. Don't overlook educational and training materials.

Ghost Writing.
No credit, just money, unless it's one of these "as told to" autobiographies.

Did you know that restaurants use "ghost writers" to publish cookbooks featuring their famous recipes?

Newspaper Column.
Easier to begin with the neighborhood paper than one of the biggies. Nothing to lose if you try to reverse the order.

Jokes.
Comedians pay for their jokes.

Comic Strip.
Recently a newcomer to the comic strip business hit the jackpot—instant syndication! He both writes and illustrates, but there are collaborators where one member of the team does the dialogue and the other, the drawings. Similar to the musical team of Rodgers and Hart.

YELLOW PAGES

Annual directories of a specialized nature are popping up and are as diverse as one on home-repair service people, a directory of professional women's services, sailboat designs, singles, bed and breakfast places, cruises, and local restaurants.

In cities that have many different ethnic populations, directories that isolate the names of residents and businesses of a single ethnic group, such as the Greek community, are in high demand.

Services from A to Z

A homebased business is where every day is Monday.

—BNF

ACCOUNTANT

Many small businesses without full-time accountants need accounting services, such as setting up record-keeping systems, doing monthly accounts, figuring taxes, and preparing profit and loss analyses.

ADVERTISING CONSULTANT OR REPRESENTATIVE

A consultant prepares an advertising strategy within the monetary budget of the client. The cost—from one hundred to very expensive dollars per month.

A representative sells ads for newspapers, magazines, television, and radio.

ADVISER

Dial-A-Decision.
One of the more unusual advisory services offered is called "Dial-A-Decision." Executives use this service for personal and professional problems. Clients buy two-hour blocks of telephone time for $400, to discuss a problem and

141

agree on a program of action to resolve it. Monthly weekend workshops are held, in groups of three or four, at $1,500 per head.

AFTER-HOURS RESCUE

What to do when the plumbing stops functioning just before three hundred wedding guests arrive for dinner at eight? This really happened to us. Fortunately our annual subscription to ''After-Hours Service'' was paid up-to-date. They provide plumbers, electricians, and any other genius a household needs to keep running, but only after other resources are closed. Any need for this business in your community?

AGENT/AGENCY

Many agents work from a home office. To give you an idea of the variety of work they perform, here is a representation: talent, real estate, insurance, annuity, literary, appraisal, promotion, licensing, music, advertising. I have a lecture agent who books appearances for me. She represents experts in different fields as well as ''personalities'' from radio, television, and movies.

ANIMAL CARE

Some of the services in demand today because pet owners just don't have the time but have the heart and the money are: dog walkers, pet-sitters, groomers, trainers, ambulance service, and animal psychologists.

I never thought I would use the services of an animal psychologist, but I did, in determining if two adult male dogs would ever learn to get along. The dog doc said they wouldn't and they didn't.

Animal Travel Agency.
Who's to growl about a minimum fee of $25 for a routine assignment like arranging shipment of a cat, plus additional fees for any other special service. In Florida, an enterpris-

ing young man is making a living on the concern of owners for their pets to travel safely. He will fly with the animal either with the carrier under the seat or in a seat alongside him.

AIRPLANE RIDES

Few of us have an airplane for an asset. A woman pilot in Los Angeles earns her living booking private passengers. When asked where her office was, she replied—"The cockpit!" She teamed up with another woman who drives a limousine for a living.

ANTHROPOLOGIST

If anthropology is your profession, home is a fine base for consultant or researcher. Land developers and land companies hire anthropologists to explore proposed sites of historical record for evidence of antiquities. The developers keep their fingers crossed that no evidence will be found so they will be allowed to build on the site.

ANTIQUES

Possible homebased businesses for you if antiques are your bag include: restorer, appraiser, broker. Stringing the beads that hang from the shades of Tiffany lamp replicas has provided one homebaser with a living for the past fifteen years.

APPRAISER

Gems, art, real estate, furniture, collectibles, antiques, weapons—whatever your specialty is, if you have sufficient expertise and keep up with current market values you can work from home as an appraiser.

AQUARIUMS

Watching fish swimming in an aquarium eases stress and may even be a means of treating high blood pressure, according to a study by the University of Pennsylvania. Sell or rent aquariums, service policy optional, to dentists and doctors for their offices, where patients have to wait and wait and wait—and their blood pressure will go down, down, down.

ARBITRAGEUR

A parklike home setting with a built-in secretary, three phones, and a telex number serves as a base for one successful international financier who simultaneously buys and sells the same or equivalent securities in order to profit from price discrepancies. It is not a business for the fainthearted.

ARCHITECT

Many architects moonlight from their homes. When they have developed enough of a private practice, they form their own companies. Some establish home offices from the start—such as Frank Lloyd Wright's Taliesin West.

ART

Convert a basement or a garage into a studio to hold private classes for the instruction of pottery making, picture framing, watercolors, oils, weaving, quilt making, stained glass, soft sculpture.

Art consultants advise clients about purchasing art objects for homes or offices.

Art dealers, representing artists and craftspeople, sell their work to private clients for homes, offices, or buildings.

ASTROLOGIST

Monthly or yearly chartings can be a natural homebased business. Astrology forecasts can be done by mail order, by appointment with clients in the home, or by phone.

AUCTIONEER

Art, estates, houses, land, furniture, horses, and many more things are sold at auctions. The "S-O-L-D TO . . ." part of the auctioneers' song is easy, but who teaches them the rest of that jargon?

AUTO DOCTOR

There's a car specialist who makes house calls called an "auto doctor." One that I've used is a Mercedes geriatrician; another solos in brakes. A specialist for electrical problems might also do well.

AUTO RESEARCHER

How I wish I had known such a service existed when I once purchased a new car. I learned what one does not see and what the salesperson omits in the sales pitch is what comes with the car. For a $175 fee, an auto researcher will act as a go-between between his client and the agencies, doing the shopping and price haggling, at delivery time will test-drive the vehicle, arranging financing if necessary, take care of registration and license plates, and even bring the paperwork to the client. Next time . . .

AUTO FOR HIRE

Many independent taxi operators put their cars to work on a twenty-four-hour basis, driving an eight- or ten-hour shift and renting the car to another driver for the next shift.

Individuals need drivers to take them to the airport, doctor, shopping, or errands. Put an ad in the classified section of the local paper and post a sign on bulletin boards about your availability.

"Sober chauffeur" is a service that will respond anytime to a call from a bar when the customer is too drunk to drive. This is the time it is prudent to be a backseat driver.

"School for chauffeurs" teaches students for six nights at $250 the differences between being a driver and a chauffeur. The class meets in the living room of the instructor. Knowledge of cardiopulmonary resuscitation is one graduation requirement.

AUTO SLEUTH

How skilled are you with engines? A former Pennsylvania garage mechanic became a forensic auto expert to provide courts with evidence of foul play or negligence. He charges from $200 to $360 per day plus expenses.

BANKBOOK RECONCILER

How many times have you heard of people who had to close a bank account and open a new one at a different bank in order to reconcile their balance? The reconciler, not an accountant, but someone who is very good at figures, will take bank statements that have been stashed away for the last year and balance them. If you can create order in somebody else's bankbook, prepare to enlarge your own bank account as soon as word gets around.

BARTENDERS

Caterers are a good resource for jobs. Because your services are generally required in the evening, other people's parties provide an income for moonlighters.

BEAUTY EXPERT

Work as a homebased makeup artist, hair conditioner and stylist, nail care expert, facial giver. Some states require licenses for these. Other possibilities for dispensing home beauty are wig and toupee maker and conditioner, color consultant, and clothes consultant.

BIBLIOTIST

An expert in determining the genuineness or authorship of handwriting, documents, and writing materials. Lends itself to homebased business very well.

BIRDS

Classes in bird-watching, bird hospital, bird boarding, selling birds. One person I know specializes in finches—and where does she keep her stock? . . . In the one-bedroom apartment, ceiling-to-floor on one of the living room walls!

BODYGUARDS AND BOUNCERS

Been working out lately? Well then, join the army of private strong arms who have cashed in on the growing insecurity of company executives, celebrities, and just plain but well-heeled folk. Both men and women trained in martial arts are hired as bouncers at parties and serve as escorts on shopping expeditions and vacations.

BOOKS

Typographer, cover designer, editor, illustrator, proofreader, publisher, consultant, author, book cover photographer: all the different talents required to produce a book can contract independently. Other possibilities include collector and dealer in vintage books, first editions as well. Book-finders track down books that are out of print for customers.

BOOKKEEPER

Entries, monthly statements, trial balances, and billing are some of the tasks small firms need. It's not enough work for a full-time bookkeeper, so they engage independent contractors by the hour or monthly fee. Depending on how many accounts you want, this can become a part-time or full-time business for you.

BROKER

Here are some examples of how varied the work of "brokers" can be: Real estate brokers can work from a home office. They may not necessarily have a sales force except for their own efforts to sell or invest in properties for themselves.

Mortgage and Loan.
High interest rates slow down the mortgage and loan departments in loan institutions, forcing the cutback or shutdown of their in-house loan officers. Many of those who fall victim to seesaw interest rates strike out on their own and work on call for different institutions from their home base.

Information Brokers.
Provide businesses with reports in changing market conditions, government regulations, competitors, and new products. Most of this information is publicly available, but it is either hard to get or, for competitive reasons, too sensitive for companies to pursue on their own. There are fewer than one dozen information "brokers" or "retailers," as they are called in the country, who act as supermarkets of information. Much of the data asked for by companies is available free at government agencies and private groups.

Fee? One info seller charges an annual retainer of $5,000 to $50,000 for special projects.

Horses.
Even four-leggeds have their own broker.

Marriage.
Bet you thought there were no more marriage brokers ex-

cept in Saudi Arabia and in *Fiddler on the Roo*
Although all the dating and singles organizations an
nesses do not promise marriage at first sight, matchmak
is big business. Some of the dating companies "fix up" one
of their offices as a living room to provide a more relaxed
setting for the meetings of the couples-to-be. You already
have that setting in your home.

Think of all ages—older people want companionship.
Specialize if you are older, in an "over fifty" club. As the
business grows, a home computer would be helpful.

BUSINESS INSTRUCTOR

Typing classes, teaching word processing, composing business letters, and whatever else the business world needs.

CAMP ADVISER

How do many parents select summer fun for their children?
They consult with someone knowledgeable about matching
children's interests to a suitable camp, or a tour in the United
States or Europe.

You could even design your own tour group and become
a pied piper.

CHILD CARE

Infant or child care, by the hour or day. Backyard nursery
school, after-school program, foster home, respite home,
child-sitting agency—for individuals and for industries who
pay for a sitter for a sick youngster so the employee can get
to the job. (See Home as a Product.)

CHILDBIRTH EDUCATOR

Teaches "pregnant couples" pre- and postnatal health care.

art and because it is, there are very few
around. Not recommended as a homebased
rida, though.

CLIPPING SERVICE

This is a business that requires only a pair of scissors and
the daily papers. The clients' instructions determine the
newspapers you subscribe to. You watch for an item that
relates to a client, then clip and file. Authors and publishers
will pay for clippings related to their books, celebrities (all
kinds), politicians, and show business folks often want to
keep track of clippings related to their careers.

CLUBS

Many special interest clubs abound. Some examples are:
Travelin' Around Town. For an annual fee a monthly trip is
planned to explore a particular section or event in the city:
historical sites, theater, or concerts.

Club Adventure on a Shoestring.
A lot of people responded to an advertisement in a newspaper for fellow "adventurers" who feel safer exploring in
groups. Numbers of people can sometimes get into special
places that individuals cannot. One such New York–based
club has two thousand members, each paying $30 per year,
plus $3 attendance and the cost of the advent, to a home-
based entrepreneur.

Weekend Adventures.
Takes a group every other weekend to a special place. These
clubs are coed, or strictly one sex, children's or adult
groups, handicapped, or by religious affiliation.

CLUB DISCOUNT

There are different kinds of discount clubs: resort, travel, restaurant, movie, theaters, bowling alleys. For an annual membership fee the member and a guest are entitled, for example, to sample a number of participating restaurants at a reduced price, or a two-for-the-price-of-one arrangement.

Your job is to decide on the kind of club; sell the idea of promotion to the participants, print membership "invitations," rent a mailing list, and send the solicitations. This type of business can be quite successful in many communities. What do you get out of it? The annual membership fees.

COLLECTION AGENCY

Not so pleasant a task, to handle the accounts of clients who insist on getting paid. You track down the delinquent accounts and dog them until they pay.

COLOR CONSULTANT

Are you Spring, Summer, Winter, or Fall? Dividing people into seasonal color types, analyzing skin tones and eye color (hair color can always be changed) to clothing, accessories, and makeup costs from $35 to $350. Color analysts are springing up around the country determined to make clients feel beautiful and happy. Watch for the dead giveaway by the bulge of cloth swatches, a constant shopping companion, in their pockets.

SCHOOL FOR COLOR CONSULTANTS

Start a living-room classroom to train others to become color analysts. One well-known authority teaches both men and women at $2,800 each for a two-week course, but not at home.

COMMODITIES ADVISER

For $33.50, you can buy one minute of consultation with an East Coast commodity trading adviser or $2,000 for an hour. If that's too steep, consider another in Montana who only charges $100 for five minutes and if both advisers are too rich a commodity for you, there are 1,998 others registered in the same field. A side note—the one in Montana raises llamas as well. (See Newsletters, under Publishing.)

COMPUTERS

The electronic revolution makes it possible to shift office work to the home. It is estimated that half of the contemporary United States labor force, fifty million strong, are electronic candidates. They are in the information industry: those people whose primary job is to move, manipulate, and/or transform information in some way or other.

With advances in telecommunications, more and more people are able to switch their work station from office to home by installing computer terminals. Office and home can be in different cities. The term "telecommuting" has been coined to denote the electronic connection between home and office. It opens up new opportunities not only for expectant and new mothers, but also for invalids. A popular alternative for those who want to cut down on commuting or avoid the commuter rat race altogether. One company reported that each employee working from home reduces monthly auto driving by five hundred miles, for a ninety dollar savings.

How It Works.
A Chicago mother left a well-paying legal secretary position to have her baby. Rather than find someone to care for her child, she combined work and child care at home. For one week she trained on a word processor at a bank, then the machine was installed in her bedroom, linked to the bank's downtown office.

At 8:30 each morning the downtown office starts transmitting the day's work. It arrives in tape form and she uses earphones to listen to the tape on her recording machine and proceeds with typing on the word-processing machine. She dispatches the material to the bank with a press of a button after dialing the bank's number and using a code number to identify herself to the computer.

She says, "It's fantastic! I save five dollars a day on gasoline needed for commuting, lunch money, clothes, and I'm home with my child."

The "electronic cottage," that's what Alvin Toffler, author of *The Third Wave*, calls the home of the not so distant future. Homebased computers are predicted to be the Ford of tomorrow. A sample of the companies using homeworkers:

Anistics Inc., Palo Alto, California
Arthur D. Little, Inc., Cambridge, Massachusetts
Lift, Inc., Northbrook, Illinois
Control Data Corporation, Minneapolis, Minnesota
Standard Oil, Indiana
First National Bank of Chicago
Montgomery Ward and Co.
Heights Information Technology Service, Tarrytown, New York, and Oakland, California
Blue Cross—Blue Shield
Continental Illinois Bank and Trust, Chicago
Walgreen's
McDonald's
Digital Equipment Corporation, Maynard, Massachusetts
Data General Corporation
A.C.S. America, New York City
American Express

COMPUTER ARTIST

You probably cannot afford to have your own computer capable of producing complex "fine art," but if you have access to a computer system, you can be a homebased computer artist—selling or distributing your work from home. The computer can be programmed to produce works of original art. The highly specialized color optics computers are rather rare, still, though there are models that draw and some have four colors. If you watch television, you are seeing computer art used in various ways, especially in commercials.

COMPUTER CONSULTANT/SYSTEMS ANALYST

Business people, financial analysts, doctors, and other professionals often baffled by technical fine points seek help to rout the myriad bugs and mysteries that plague new systems, as well as to determine the kind of system to install. Individual computer buffs, once their purchase is installed, are confused by the instructions and need an interpreter to assist. The consultant makes a house call or as many as needed for tutoring. One fancy department store offered in their Christmas catalog the ultimate gift—$500 of computer consulting.

The leading computer companies, often criticized for lack of follow-up assistance for the customer, need referrals of specific people to assist.

COMPUTER HOME PARTIES

One of the newest entries in the multilevel selling businesses are computers. Home computers have joined the ranks of must-have-in-the-home equipment such as food processors, microwave ovens, and video gadgets. A distributor or a representative demonstrates and sells a particular brand of computer to a group of people gathered together by the party host. Living rooms are a more relaxing place to buy.

COMPUTER MAGAZINES/BOOKS/NEWSLETTERS

Books about computers are elbowing out cookbooks as number one best-sellers. The new target in this special interest market is for the children to have their own publications. There are 24 million children between the ages of ten and sixteen, many of whom will use computers in the next few years. The market looks lucrative.

COMPUTER OPERATOR

Home-computer owners around the country started bulletin boards to store and receive information and messages for thousands of other home-computer owners. Bulletin board technology has business applications in mail order, for example, bypassing central computers as well as the United States Postal Service to distribute electronic mail. Special interest groups use the boards to exchange information about genealogy, astronomy, commodities, medical questions. There's still plenty of room for you in this burgeoning industry.

COMPUTER REPAIR TECHNICIAN

By the end of this decade the Bureau of Labor Statistics forecasts that 172,000 jobs will be available for mechanics to keep the computers operating.

COMPUTER SCHOOL

Can a classroom be set up in your home? For adults or children? One company charges $5,000 to $25,000 to train disabled persons and, I believe, federal funds assist that program.

COMPUTER SOFTWARE WRITER

People buy machines for what they can do. The value of a computer lies in its software. A programmer types on a computer terminal a minutely specific set of instructions, which are recorded on a small disk. When "played" in the computer's disk drive, the software instantly reprograms the computer to perform a function the user wants, from calculating the hour of sunrise to writing a letter. Does that help to remove some of the mystique?

One high-school dropout scaled to the heights of computerland, earning as a programmer a six-figure income in royalties last year. It's a business a physically handicapped person might want to consider. The number of homebound computer writers and operators is small but growing.

CONSULTANT

There are consultants for just about every field today—in management, life-enhancement (planning for retirement), career (like me), jury, tax, divorce, health, assertion training, computer, restaurant, financial, industrial time management, productivity, investment, book/magazine/newsletter publishing, and on and on and on. The consultant acts as an adviser, analyzing the problems, and making recommendations. The consultant works by the job, on an hourly or daily basis, or on a yearly retainer.

CONTRACTOR

Some specialized services provided are cleaning, building, painting, electrical, plumbing, roofing. Kinds of residential and commercial services offered include cleaning and maintenance, building, plumbing, painting, or roofing. A contractor can do the work but generally hires employees, buys materials per job, and stores materials in the garage or basement if necessary.

A woman who began a cleaning service by doing the work herself now has forty-six employees and grosses $4 million a year. (See Home Maintenance.)

CONVENTION PLANNER

Companies engage outside planners to develop programs, plan menus, and handle logistics. Special spouse programs are no longer geared to the stay-at-home wife but to the growing number of males in attendance and employed wives. (See Meeting Planners).

COOKING CLASSES

Adults.
University-sponsored cooking classes have used home kitchens for many of their classes. If the class is held in your kitchen and a teacher is provided, you pay no tuition charges, and a rental fee is paid to you. If you are the cook-

156

ing teacher, too, you are paid a salary. Sponsor your own class in Thai, vegetarian, cake-decorating, bread-making, jam-making—anything you feel you do well.

Children.
Hold a class on Saturday mornings. Parents are eager for their children to learn more about nutrition and to take over in their kitchens. Instead of kids asking "What are we going to do today?" the tables will turn when parents ask *them* "When are we going to eat; we're hungry!"

When a teacher of Japanese cooking passed around the fish cakes, tiny pickled plums, shiny sushi, and egg pancakes to his class of six thirteen-year-olds, the reactions were "Ooh, yuck," or "Gross." Yet when class was over, they bragged to their parents about their newly acquired Japanese cooking skills and the benefits of tofu.

COSMETOLOGIST

Your sink or mine. Haircuts generally cost less if the customer is willing to bend over a kitchen sink or bathtub for a hairwash. That's one attraction of a homebased haircutter: another is a more peaceful snip than at one of those hectic salons. Balding men reluctant to display their concern openly seek more privacy with their scalp massages and magic formula treatments.

If your scissors are willing to make house and office calls, busy professionals, executives, invalids depend on the traveling beauticians. Don't forget to figure travel costs into your price.

COSTUMER

Specialize in period apparel. Put on shows for women's clubs, museums. Make elaborate masks and costumes for Mardi Gras, Halloween festivals, and performers both human and animal.

COUNSELOR

In one sense of the word, "counselor" has been synonymous with "lawyer." People who give advice, a plan of action or behavior for clients in other than legal matters, as in psychological counseling, are also called *counselors*.

Drug and alcohol problems of employees have become a major concern to corporations, so much so that counselors are hired to help individual employees.

COURIER SERVICE

In the basement office of a Chicago town house is a $1 million-dollar courier business begun by a lawyer who also is a private consultant. Diversifying pays off here by providing three incomes.

DATING SERVICE

There are many angles to these services. One concept was originated by two women who dreamed up monthly posh events where singles could mix. It's the "poshness" that draws the crowds; some of the parties cost the single as much as $200.

Poor little rich girl wants to meet poor little rich man. How? A dating service for millionaires. She pays, he pays, $100,000 to meet.

Certainly after these two original successful ideas for a dating service you can come up with your own angle for meeting, mixing, and matching.

DOG TRAINER

If you have a way with dogs, can get some classes and experience at training them, the following might be the sort of advertising you would do:

"Don't give away your unmannerly pet. I will housebreak your pet, will stop pet's digging up the yard, running away, eating your steak when your back is turned. Antisocial behavior corrected or your money back. House calls only."

DIRECT MAIL SERVICE

This service sells mailing lists for specific populations. Some companies will also affix the address labels and mail. Some will keep your mailing list up-to-date if you furnish them with new addresses, change of addresses.

EDUCATION CONSULTANT

An educational consultant (like me) or adviser or counselor helps clarify career goals and plan a college program, select an appropriate school for a client, taking into consideration psychological needs, financial picture, and responsibilities.

ENVELOPES

"Stuffing envelopes" ads can be a rip-off. If you answer an ad claiming that "thousands" can be earned at home by stuffing envelopes if you send $10, $15, or $20 for a kit, don't. It's supposed to work like a pyramid game.

ESCORT AGENCY

This is a *legitimate* companionship arrangement for people—men or women—who want to go out for an evening, or to the races, but do not want to go alone. Many women in "high society" have used paid escorts for years. And why not? The escorts are carefully screened by the agency and booked as needed. Do not confuse this service with the gigolo or call girl business. Strictly male order.

EXERCISE STUDIO

I have gone to an exerciser who individualizes, prescribes, and supervises body movements. The living room of the exerciser's house has been converted to a small, efficient gym. Is she expensive? Yes. Is her business in demand? Yes, because there are enough people who prefer private to group instruction. You can cater to both if there's enough space.

Outfit a van into a traveling gym and muscle right over to client's house. Fitness-on-wheels program for home delivery.

EXPEDITER

Anyone who has gone through the hassle of getting a building permit from City Hall knows the worth of hiring someone who will take care of dealing with the bureaucracy.

FASHION CONSULTANT

Love to shop? Shop away and spend someone else's money. A fashion consultant may get a request to evaluate others' wardrobes and advise them what to buy or help with an image change. Some consultants stress that they save their clients' money by coordinating outfits. Some clients just don't care to shop or have no time to shop, but must have twelve pairs of assorted shoes for fall—size 8B, please.

FIX-IT

There are many kinds of specialized repairing: caning, watch, camera, handbag, luggage, electrical appliances, jewelry, plumbing, television, radios, and on and on. Depending on the kind of repair service, customers can drop off the articles at your house, or you can go to their house.

FOLK HEALER

Voodoo healers, rootworkers, and spirit mediums have no licenses and many do not have a grade school education, but now many psychologists and mental health clinics accept them openly as colleagues. Folk healing is widespread and is in all ethnic groups. Rough estimates put the numbers of folk healers of all sorts in the tens of thousands. About 80 percent of all episodes of mental and physical illness in the United States are handled by home remedies or folk cures.

These folk healers create hope, same as psychotherapists do; they provide patients with acceptance. Virtually every one of the many ethnic cultures has one or more varieties of folk healing tradition, including the voodoo of the Haitians, the santería of the Cubans, the espiritismo of the Puerto Ricans, the charismatic faith healers among white groups, the rootworkers and other spiritualists among different black groups, and dozens of others.

Positive expectancy, the belief that it will work, is not only the key to a healer's success with a patient but also a key to the success of your homebased business.

FOOD STYLIST

Ever wonder why your cookin' never quite looks like the food photos in magazines? If you used all the sprays and props a food stylist does and all that time in arrangement, Grandma's apple pie recipe would be just as gorgeous—but not edible.

FORTUNE-TELLER

Reveal the future through tea leaves, tarot cards, crystal ball, reading palms. Also good for party bookings.

FREIGHT TRAFFIC CONSULTANT

Advises independent truckers on current regulations, audits freight bills, provides safety patrols for the larger companies to check on adherence to driving policies. A former employee, now a freight controller, teamed with his wife and two sons and six phone lines in their own homebased business. Going from a $22,500 salary to $500,000 yearly income can happen to others willing to take the risk.

FUND-RAISER

A professional fund-raiser can work independently for organizations: profit-making, nonprofit, or political. Many people have had lots of experience as ''volunteers'' for community organizations. Now they are applying those skills professionally (which means they are now getting paid).

FUNERAL DIRECTOR

To many, home is for every body, caskets stored in the basement, services and offices on first floor, "living" quarters on the second.

GARAGE SALES

Green-grassed front yards, once the pride of the owner, have gone the way of inflation. Garage sales and flea markets are not confined to garages anymore, spreading onto front lawns, back porches, stretching into weekdays, rather than being a Sunday-only business. Merchandise need not be your own but can be purchased from another flea market or a cooperative venture among friends. And, in fact, you can go away when the sale is on if you hire a garage sale promoter to do the work for you. Although *Fortune* magazine would not consider this business worthy of a mention, livings are made or supplemented by the sales.

My favorite ongoing sale is held on the front lawn of a Los Angeles home on a busy city cross street for the past six years. I've watched it grow from a one-front-lawn to a two-front-lawn business plus an open garage that reveals a nursery of plants. The tanned, sailor-capped entrepreneur sits outside in his canvas director's chair, taking in the money from the crowds he draws. Mastercard is accepted.

GARDENER

Specialize in an organic approach to gardening and advertise yourself as one who:

> Takes the ducks along
> To eat the snails
> Which ate the flowers
> That you planted

For the customer
Who insists on
Strictly organic.

A route is easy to establish—just let one house that you work on become the envy of the neighbors.

Give lessons or demonstrations to garden club members in yours or someone else's backyard. Teach bonsai, animal-shaped shrubbery, rose or orchid care, landscaping, indoor plant care, and so on. If you have a green thumb, it can be profitable to share your expertise.

GENEALOGIST

Remember everyone's sudden interest in their "roots"? This vocation has grown into a flowering business. Some tracers of lost relations have added to their sales with custom-designed family pennants, seals, crests, plaques, scrolls, and awards.

GIFT SELECTION SERVICE

If you have always enjoyed shopping, this one is a natural. For example, the client may be an individual who may want you to select six gifts within a specified price range, gift-wrap, and deliver. Corporations and smaller companies, busy professional people, and executives use this convenience. It does not mean that you keep a large inventory of stock. Make wholesale contacts and buy as needed. You become a gift detective.

GOFER

Americans are paying to make life easier—$549.2 million for services in 1980! Gofers call themselves: Rent-a-Wife, Let Me Do It, Hire-a-Service, Surrogate Wife, Brains for Lease, Leg Work, Rent-a-Fairy-Godmother. Some of the kinds of services they give are:

Running interference, waiting for the service person to

come. Busy careerists do not want to waste away their time, so they hire stand-ins.

Returning something to a department store.

Accepting deliveries.

Chauffeuring to and from the airport, taking the dog to the vet, children to dancing classes.

Buying clothes, gifts, groceries to keep the refrigerator well-stocked. Some gofers will even cook and freeze enough food for the weekly menu.

Secretarial—paying your bills, typing, making appointments, reporting complaints.

GOPHERS

Setting traps to catch gophers for timid homeowners who have despaired of their Swiss-cheese lawns. Have you read about the children of one family who made so much money from catching gophers for neighbors that the state wants to collect taxes?

Removing unwanted beehives is another nuisance-remover service. You must be trained in order to do both these services safely.

GRANTMANSHIP

Grants totaling more than $100,000 a year are offered by each of some 3,100 foundations in the country; $2.5 billion given away by corporations; $2.4 billion by foundations; $85 billion in federal grants; individual giving—$39.9 billion in 1980. Your job is to pry dollars from the target foundation for clients, usually nonprofit organizations. Also, you can teach seminars in grantmanship.

GRAPHOLOGIST

Studies handwriting for the purpose of character analysis. Private clients or services are used by some corporations to screen employees.

GREETINGS

How do you like your happy birthdays?

Remember Western Union's original singing telegram? If you do, that will date you, but their enterprise led the way for many entries into the greeting business. You can specialize in messages conveyed by an animal of the customer's choice. A playful gorilla or a horse, lion, or teddy bear sings a message to someone's love. For an extra charge, a gift of matching stuffed animal is included.

Tap dancing, and dance messengers, or Cupids bringing flowers and candy are popular. Bet you did not know that the song "Happy Birthday to You" is a copyrighted song. If sung by a messenger for commercial gain, the company using the messenger, if caught, is subject to royalty payments.

Reminding people to *send* the greeting is a service business. It operates in two ways: the client gives you the list of names and dates to be remembered. You send a reminder card to the client a week before the due date. Or you keep track, as well as send the gift.

To send bouquets of long-stemmed helium balloons is a delightful, happy, fashionable greeting business, involving a small investment other than advertising, no spoilage; all you need are balloons in assorted colors, a tank of helium, colorful ribbons, and a means of transportation, and you are in business. Would you believe that you can even buy a balloon franchise? (See Balloons, under Products.)

GUIDE

Destination: adventure and beauty. One ad reads: "Not to worry. Hire a wildflower guide who will hop into your car and direct you to the best of the floral displays. Charges $15 per hour for a rented naturalist." Another, 4-Wheel Drive Desert All-Day Tours charges $75 per couple or $35 a person for four passengers. Then there's the Camping Delux, an outfit that pampers with roomy tents, gourmet meals, even swats the mosquitoes. Foreign tour groups hire guides who speak their language in the cities visited or to accompany the group across the country.

HEADHUNTER

A headhunter is someone who finds the right executive with the specified qualifications for a company. The headhunter can be a one-person agency, can specialize in a specific field such as real estate or electronics or can generalize. The company pays a high commission, usually a percentage of the first-year's salary paid to the executive. How do you find the potential candidates? Usually they are wooed away from another company.

How do you get the clients, the companies? The same way. All businesses grow, through communication. Call by phone, in person, by mail, attend seminars and meetings, to get yourself known as a headhunter.

This business was once a male preserve, but now over two hundred executive research firms have female recruiters. So women join the "old-girl" network. The pay is good. Ask the "old-boys"!

HEALTH SERVICES

Any of the professional medical services—doctor; dentist; midwife; psychologist; chiropractor; marriage, family, or child counselor—can work from an office in the home. Many patients prefer a home office to an office building because they feel more relaxed there. Many physical therapists, masseuses, skin and hair care consultants, yoga teachers, and childbirth educators conduct their businesses from home.

In Minnesota, ailing people flock to the door of a man who practices the art of healing. No charge—just a plate for donations.

Have you been to a vitamin party lately? Individuals selling vitamins is a sideline that has caught on.

HOME NURSING AGENCY

Finding someone to care for an invalid patient at home is not an easy task. That problem gave a couple an idea of supplying personnel around the clock: a companion, LVN, RN, or homemaker for the individual case. This agency bills the patient directly, but many nurses' referral agencies charge only for the name of someone to help.

Travel Nurse.
Have thermometer, will travel? This is one way to enjoy a luxurious floating home and to get paid to go to the Greek Isles!

HOME MAINTENANCE

Agency.
For an annual fee, names of experienced, licensed workers for residential needs or maintenance are provided. All workers are screened. Usually names in about thirty fields of home maintenance are on file, recommended by friends or by word of mouth.

Service.
A woman started her own business in the northwest with $35, gumption, and a good idea. Her Dial-a-Mop is a house-cleaning service. She found people all over the country wanted to duplicate her success, so she wrote a how-to book. Turned down by publishers, she had it printed herself, selling at $50 per copy. She says: *"There's a whole lot of mythology about small business that scares people away. You can be an ordinary person with a lot of drive, a good idea, and some smarts about how to market it."* (See Contractor.)

HOTEL/MOTEL CONSULTANT

Women seem to be more selective than men in regard to hotel accommodations. Advising management how to provide special security and comfort for the growing number of traveling businesswomen is important to the hotel industry.

HOUSE INSPECTOR

A thorough house inspection can help a home buyer avoid a costly mistake or provide the ammunition needed to persuade the seller to lower the price or make the repairs. The

American Society of Home Inspectors has four hundred members.

HUMILIATION HEALER

A new industry has started up to save the victims of embarrassment. One example is the problem of too many traffic tickets; another example is having your car towed away because you parked illegally. The next step for you in both these situations may be time-consuming, embarrassing, and highly inconvenient. Now, for a yearly membership fee and with a valid major credit card, a telephone call to Humiliation Elimination, Inc. will solve your problem. A chauffeured limousine stocked with champagne and caviar will pick you up and take you to claim your impounded car—or an employee of H.E. will claim it while you wait in the limo.

HYPNOTIST

No amateurs, please. Reputable hypotists charge anywhere from $25 to $75 per session and work to help people with all sorts of problems.

IMAGE CONSULTANT

Companies are more concerned with the "right" look in hard times than in good times. Keener competition forces executives to spruce up. The number of image-maker firms is increasing rapidly because people are increasingly concerned about how they are perceived by others. They worry about their diction, their speech-writing and delivery, how to make effective presentations, even how to arrive at the best hairstyle and color and the most flattering makeup. Videotapes are widely used in this work.

INSTRUCTION

The Living Room Classroom is a new concept that's flourishing. One-day seminars or a series on a single subject matter are taught in the instructor's home or one of the students'. Its success is because charges are generally less than extension programs at universities and colleges, homelike atmosphere is friendlier and less hassle than trying to find a parking space at a campus lot, and the program offers a way to meet people who share a common interest. Some entrepreneurs have put together a network of classes, publish a catalog, advertise, and offer the teacher a 50/50% split on the amount collected.

Teach bridge, chess, card-memory techniques for blackjack, backgammon, Cardiopulmonary Resusitation (CPR), self-defense, Spanish, computers, and so on.

If you have a pool, give swimming lessons, or charge rent for a teacher to have use of the pool for students.

"Have tennis racket. Can teach," and if you have a tennis court, rent it.

Classes in home maintenance are popular owing to the high cost of plumbers, electricians, wallpapering, and . . .

Puppetry, magic, cooking, makeup, needlepoint, flower arrangement, etc.

One kind of instruction for children I find amusing (yet enough parents take it seriously to make a profitable business) is teaching etiquette to children. Manners is the name of the game here. One teacher charges $3,000 (no typographical error) for a series of eight lessons, with graduation dependent on passing "which is the fish fork" exam!

Car Repair.
A mechanic whose customers come from far distances because of his outstanding work also gives Saturday morning classes in basic car repair. Don't know if his baking talents outdo his teaching abilities—he serves homemade cookies after class.

Public Speaking.
Teach public speaking skills, or as it is sometimes called, performance dynamics. These skills are in high demand by the executive set. Videotapes are effective teaching tools for this.

School for Butlers.
In England a new school has been founded with twelve students enrolled, learning the art of "butlering." The graduates, after six months rigorous training, are exported to American millionaires. We could use our own school in the U.S.

P.S. Apprenticing as a helper to the teacher is a way of learning a skill or brushing up on one that has been dormant for a number of years, and it's always helpful (even if you are an expert) to learn how others perform.

INTERIOR DESIGNER

The majority of interior designers freelance from home base, designing for businesses, including hotels and also private residences. Custom designs and/or furniture can be purchased from catalogs. There are many books and classes available to help prepare you for this career.

IRONER

This deserves a special listing. As increasing numbers of women began to work outside the home, one of the first indulgences they allowed themselves was to get someone else to do the ironing. There's no mechanical device such as dishwashers to do the job, except to escape to drip-dry clothing. So, if you like to watch the soaps and you are a good ironer, combine the two and you've got yourself a business. "The Iron Maiden" outgrew the house and had to find a commercial location.

LEARNING SKILLS CENTER

Teach learning skills for children in your home, both handicapped and nonhandicapped, who need extra help with their schoolwork. Bright children, too, who do not work up to their capabilities and need after-school special attention to change and improve their study habits. (See listing under Tutor.)

LIBRARIAN

Sets up, organizes, catalogs books for private persons, business, and industry. Advises and makes new acquisitions.

LIMOUSINE SERVICE

Tell your clients to leave the driving to you. One plush car and a continuous advertisement could beget, in time, a stable of vehicles.

LOST-AND-FOUND SLEUTH

Credit Cards.
For $12 per year one company will have all lost credit cards canceled as soon as they are reported lost and will reissue new ones.

Tracer of Lost Persons.
This confidential service is used for runaways, spouse or child, adopted persons who want to know their birth parents, old sweethearts, misplaced relatives.

Animal Detective.
When dogs and cats are lost, stolen, or have strayed away, many people are more apt to get help to find their missing pet than a relative. Ask Sherlock Bones.

Car Gone.
Towed-away or stolen Mercedes, Porsches, even Chevrolets are brought back to grieving owners by private investigators. No guarantees that the Blaupunkt radio, the motor, and the tires will be returned—clients may get only the skeleton of their beloved auto. However, seems like a natural for a homebased business if you've got a nose for missing autos.

The Book Sleuth.
I guess because I like books so well that this livelihood has particular appeal. A one-woman business on the East Coast specializes in finding out-of-print children's books. Her di-

verse clientele ranges from clients seeking rare first editions to favorite books from childhood memories. All are willing to pay from $10 to more than $1,000 for a book that might originally have sold for a quarter. She advertises her services in *The New York Times Book Review*. Last year more than four hundred readers used her services. All this from a small office in her home.

MARRIAGE

The Ceremony.
A part-time minister earns a part-time living devising computer weddings for couples who prefer to keypunch their "I do's." The Reverend defends computerized ceremonies as modern marriage. A far cry from Lady Di's and Prince Charles's nuptials.

In the computer hopper is a marriage-counseling program for those whose quickie "I do" becomes "I won't." And if this programmed software fails, an unwedding program, a digital divorce, is available.

Custom (noncomputerized) Weddings.
These custom weddings have been homebased businesses for many Reno and Las Vegas clergy.

Bridal Clothes.
At discount prices or rental of formal finery.

Transportation: Horse and Carriage or Limousine?
You don't have to own them yourself. You have to know the resources to provide the mode of transportation. Wedding clients have been known to request anything from a double-decker London Bus to a Sicilian-donkey–drawn wagon.

The Place.
Does your house lend itself for wedding parties? Rent the setting, provide the trimmings, and afterward be prepared to sweep up the rice.

Classified Ad Marriage Bureau.
"If you want to meet interesting, professional, intelligent

people who are marriage-minded, call 000-LOVE." A two-line ad and you are in business.

MEDIATOR

Interest in divorce mediation is mushrooming. The president of the 1,200-member Academy of Family Mediators predicts that within five years, half of the divorces in the United States will be mediated not litigated. Mediation offers divorcing couples a means of making joint decisions without slugging it out in court.

There are a few associations and universities that offer instruction. It's a natural for those with social service experience with families.

MEETING PLANNER

As annual meetings of salespeople, franchise holders, and dealers become more expensive and less productive, a growing number of companies are turning to outside specialists to handle the complete package, from airline ticketing to whatever happens during the gathering. The specialists help management to be brief by writing their speeches and coaching. It isn't unusual for a company to spend $300,000 for a three-day meeting for two hundred people.

MIDWIFE

There is a return to natural childbirth and midwives. Men and women have entered this field. You may want to check with your state regulations about licensing.

In traveling around the country speaking to audiences about homebased business I met a midwife whose patients are DOGS. Nervous owners arrange for her services and postbirth care for the new mothers. *That* business was a new one for me.

MODEL

One housewife earns $400 for eighteen hours of showing lingerie in sophisticated bars. Part-time and full-time modeling pays well and if you become famous, you can earn a bundle! Get attached to one of the modeling agencies, if you can.

MUSIC

Going to the music teacher's house is another of those old-time traditions. Instrument or voice instruction, consultant work, soundproof recording studios, lyric writing, and composing present no neighborhood problems, but drum lessons do.

If you sing solo parts in church choirs, a fee is customary. You should be paid.

Seventy percent of the three hundred thousand members of the American Federation of Musicians are part-timers. Form a combo, and earn extra income playing the bagpipes, jazz, rock, chamber music, or western music. Book yourselves at private parties, clubs, summer music festivals. One established group I know includes a bank president, a doctor, a college professor, and a business executive.

There are also consultants and collectors of antique music and instruments.

NEEDLE ARTS INSTRUCTION

The state of womanly arts today is for cash. Don't mean to be sexist about needlework but women have had a long history of providing warmth, creating beautiful garments and furnishings for their families and yours. Now handknits, quilts, needlepoint, and tapestries are enjoying a rebirth for collectors and appreciators of these artists.

Everyone's knitting. A handknit sweater is high fashion but costly. An expert I know makes her living giving knitting instructions, about $10 for a sweater pattern and $25 to put it together. You don't have to go to Ireland to buy the popular Irish handknits. In a needle art magazine ad some smart person will send an Irish sweater pattern for $3.

NOTARY

Have you tried to find a notary lately? A disappearing service.

NEWSPAPER DISTRIBUTOR

Are you up anyway from 5:00 a.m. to 9:00 a.m.? Supervise and/or distribute morning newspapers, or the afternoon paper.

NUTRITIONIST

Help people with weight control by planning their special diets, and/or functioning as a nutrition consultant. A well-known nutritionist supplies the groceries as well, to keep the clients out of markets, removing a source of temptation and extra pounds.

PARTY PLANNER

You name it, they do it or they create one for you, every last detail, and you are a guest at your own party. The necessary staff can be contracted per party or maintained on a permanent basis as the business grows.

Two such women joined together in a venture from home called "Rent a Grandma." That concept evolved into party arranging, and the grandmas handle everything. Today they are in a solid financial position, well-established, and turn down any party under $1,000.

PARTY SERVER

Let's say you like to cook for the party but kitchen duty leaves you missing all the fun. Hire a server. I have used the same woman for the past twenty years. The only problem is for holidays she is so popular, she's booked a year ahead.

PIANO MOVER

Piano movers are specialists in the moving business.

PIANO TUNER

Almost as hard to find as chimney sweeps. Though there are some books on the subject, apprenticing is the best way to learn this work. It may take time to build up a clientele, but if you're good, you've got them for the duration.

PHOTOGRAPHER

What parents can resist a picture of their child astride a real pony. The intinerant photographer and his sleek pony has never left us. Even in hard times it is difficult to say no to him.

Portraits, parties, weddings, heritage houses, commercial. Specialize or generalize, or teach it. Offer your stock of photos to photo research agencies, magazines, book publishers, and newspapers.

PICNIC PRO

(See Super Sports.)

PLANT TENDER

Plant tender service is on a contract basis with homes, banks, offices, hotel lobbies. A natural for green thumb enthusiasts. In this growing service, there are plant hospitals where the patient is boarded with you for better or worse. One word of caution: investigate how crowded the field is in your area before deciding to compete.

POLITICS

There's always an election coming up at the local, state, or national level. Conduct telephone field surveys for politicians, candidates, political issues, special interest groups.

One woman who ran a field survey service became so engrossed in the political scene, she ran for office, and won!

P.O. BOXES

An investment banker runs his own post office with one employee. As a moonlighter, he expects his $20,000 investment to provide 20 percent of his income next year.

He thought up the idea, like many entrepreneurs do, because he was disgusted with his own personal mail delivery and decided he was going to offer other consumers an alternative.

Are you fed up and not going to take it anymore? You know it can apply to other services besides the mail.

PROMOTER

Garage Sales.
Want to organize garage sales? Garage sale promoters do it all: organize, price, advertise, sell for a flat fee or a percentage of the gross sales.

Game Show Prize Promotion.
The task is to convince manufacturers, resorts, restaurants, and airlines that their contributions go to their own worthy cause—low-cost advertising.

PROPERTY MANAGER

Get your rent free and a salary by managing an apartment house. Or form a property management company to rent, refurbish, and maintain clients' properties.

PSYCHIC

Who knows where your long-gone Aunt Mildred hid the jewels? A psychic knows—that's who! Some police departments enlist the assistance of psychics to help solve crimes.

PUBLIC RELATIONS

This communication service represents and acts as a liaison between the client and the media, and provides marketing service. The client can be an individual or a company. Dream up fund-raising events for nonprofit organizations, politicians, stores, etc.

RELOCATION AGENT

This is a relatively new service of assisting the transferred employee to settle down in a new community. Although inflation has crimped the pocketbooks of some companies in the practice of transferring as many employees as they were doing, there's still quite a bit of action. Corporate transfers from Canada to the United States alone in 1980 were 9,500 families. Contact corporations and offer complete relocation services, including unpacking and stocking the refrigerator before the relocated family arrives.

A growing number of executives are trying to hold on to the old homestead and their low-interest mortgages. So instead of selling when transferred, a property management firm is hired to find tenants and take care of repairs and other details. The fee, up to $2,000 per year, is usually paid by the executive's company.

Helping the relocated spouse to find a job is another developing need. The career advancement was just too good to pass up, so what's a husband to do in a new city with no job? Companies will assist by making available to the spouse a relocation job consultant.

REMAIL SERVICE

For unusual reasons, individuals and businesses sometimes want postmarks to be other than their native city.

RENT-A-_____

Whatever the customer needs, you get it: furniture, guest for a party, car, villa in Morocco, speaker for a meeting.

RENT-A-CELEBRITY

Try this one for an exciting homebased business. Dolly Parton or Mae West—take your pick. I've seen the Dolly Parton facsimile. She arrived at a dinner party while guests were still lingering over coffee, a rip-roaring, pink-satined messenger of love. Her ten-minute repartee including a bawdy song, an oversize chocolate kiss for male guests, and a puckery kiss for the host. Her exit, as brash and noisy as her entrance had been, left the guests in hysterics. The little show biz interlude costs $125 and lasts about ten minutes.

Unemployed actors and stunt experts jump from cakes at banquets, as belly dancers, as female impersonators, for fantasy fulfillment, publicity stunts, or just for fun.

RENT-A-NATURALIST

Will act as a guide to nature's natural wonders, whatever they may be, in the part of the world you are visiting—$15 an hour, four hours minimum.

RENT-A-SHEEP

Help stop noise pollution and save energy. Use sheep to keep lawns and hillsides baa-utiful. Will deliver. Hard to believe but this business provides a substantial income for a retired couple.

RENT-A-SUITCASE

The luggage lender appeals to the infrequent traveler, renters with little storage space, or those who want to show off elegant suitcases but can't afford to make the purchase. Rent sturdy Pullmans ($1.45 to $1.75 a day), luggage carts (35 cents a day), hanging bags ($1.30 a day), animal carriers, voltage converters, and travel irons.

RENT-A-TABLECLOTH

A mother-and-daughter team make their own stock of colorful cloths, napkins, bed linens. The daughter works a nine-to-five job. Because the business is growing so rapidly she plans to quit to devote her full attention to the Linen Lenders. The rental fee includes laundering after use.

RENT-A-TOOL

A twenty-three-year-old woman earns $25,000 a year stocking all kinds of tools for rent. She got the idea when friends and neighbors were forever borrowing from her initially small collection of tools. Obviously she disregarded Shakespeare when he has Polonius advise "neither a borrower nor lender be . . ."

RESEARCHER

Doctoral and master's degree candidates seek help in gathering their data. Lawyers use researchers to go through the microfiche at law libraries and the legal documents at Hall of Records. Many other professions and companies use researchers.

RESTORER

Restoration of fine works of art, family heirlooms, antique and classic cars, houses, and pianos.

REUNION PRO

Fewer alumni have the time to locate old high school graduates for the class reunion, so today professional firms are taking on such tasks. One company retains more than fifty freelance researchers just to track down lost alumni. Because these pros are paid by the body count of located alumni, the affairs are better attended. The planners receive up-front money for such costs as postage and caterer deposits. The profits range from $4 to $10 a head.

ROOMMATE-FINDING SERVICE

High rents and house payments have caused singles, divorcés, students, and older persons to double or triple up. Would-be condominium and house owners are now looking for congenial investment-partners as roommates because they cannot swing the down payment and monthly costs by themselves.

SECRETARY-TYPIST

A national home typists network is designed to encourage at-home typists to gather informally every few months to discuss problems ranging from where to buy supplies to how to deal with difficult clients.

The five major markets for typing are academic, business or commercial, medical (including doctors, hospitals, and clinics), legal, manuscripts and scripts (the writing field). In Hollywood, a specialized typing service works twenty-four hours a day getting scripts ready for the next day's filming.

Small companies farm out their work on a pick-up-and-deliver basis because they cannot afford or do not need a full-timer.

You can begin by typing theses, dissertations, résumés, correspondence, school papers, and manuscripts. Post a notice on school bulletin boards. Place ads in college newspapers and send your business cards to instructors.

SELF-DEFENSE

Classes held in private homes on learning how to use tear gas or Mace, and other defense tactics, are the new kind of "house party." Teaching karate to adults or children is in high demand.

SEMINARS

If you have specialized knowledge in fields such as management, weight control, computers, owning your own business, import/export, executive secretary, human sexuality, problem-solving, assertiveness training, legal or accounting changes in rules, tax laws—to name a few—conduct your own seminar. I do. My subject matter? Home-based businesses, of course.

Or, take the initiative and approach a company you think may need your services. Corporations often hire outside experts to bring their employees up-to-date.

SEWING EXPERT

A bread-and-butter business is this one: alterations, tailoring, dressmaking, one of the oldest ways to earn an extra income from home. Stock some fabric in the closet for the customer who cannot go to a fabric store. Make house calls.

Home sewing classes have made a comeback because people can't afford to buy ready-made clothing. A woman's well-made two-piece summer suit selling for $100 or so in a department store costs about $40 on a do-it-yourself basis. Also, the quality of ready-to-wear items just isn't what it used to be.

Teach children and adult classes on how to sew, and for graduation put on a fashion show at an organization luncheon to promote students for the next series of classes.

SEX THERAPIST

A Ph.D. or M.D. who helps patients with problems related to their sexuality or sexual relationships.

SITTER

It used to be people would engage a sitter for their children, but then when veterinarians claimed animals fare better when left in familiar surroundings, animal lovers began to earn money as sitters. Now add house sitters to the list. Owners are afraid their plants will die off if unwatered and/or their possessions will be missing on their return. Sitting is great for moonlighters.

SHOPPER

Like bargains? Parisian bargains? For twenty years an American living in Paris has provided inside information to tourists. For $350 a day, she leads visitors to bargain stores. Or just give her your shopping list.

SPACE PLANNER/ORGANIZER

Homes and offices are using the services of expert organizers for achieving order to function effectively. People are always fighting against clutter. Do you have a natural talent for space utilization?

SOAPS

Soaps are such big business that they deserve their own separate heading.

Star Attraction.
An interesting idea is using soap-opera "stars" to promote shopping malls, amusement parks, sports tournaments, fairs, grand openings. This promotion agent contracts with management, contracts the performers, arranges for their transportation and lodging, and also can act as the master/mistress of ceremonies.

What kinds of promotional ideas can you think up that might be marketable? You can begin with your own neighborhood shopping center, and think what would draw more customers to the merchants, sell them the concept, and take care of the arrangements.

Call-for-Soap.
Some people can't stand missing an episode, so, for $25 for a three-month period, they can call and find out what is happening on a soap. Customers get a special four-digit code number and are entitled to three calls a day. This unique service has gone national. Who would have ever thought it could be a success!

SOCIAL GRACES INSTRUCTOR

There are people who make a living teaching others—from corporate executives to teenagers to just ordinary folk who want to learn the proper amenities—how to read and order from a French menu, from a wine list, which fork to use, and so on.

SPEECH PATHOLOGIST

Works with children and adults with speech disorders. Voice training for public speaking is done by these specialists. Often they work through schools, hospitals, but private practice from home is a natural.

SPIRITUALIST

Outer-world communicator, "reunites the separated." Individual consultation or group séance. Out-of-this world party entertainment.

STOCKBROKER

A broker who executes orders to buy and sell securities and also often acts as a security dealer.

STORYTELLER

Reviving an old art, about 2,700 years in existence, around the country and in Canada, enthusiasts are setting up storytelling libraries, holding storytelling festivals, and establishing storytelling schools. Skilled storytellers are in hot demand by adults as well as children. Does it pay? Yes, it does—$500 for an hour and a half performance. There's a school in Toronto specializing in teaching storytelling.

SUPER SPORTS

Want employees to let their hair down, drop the barriers that separate bosses from underlings? Hire someone to stage organized wacky sports events for the company picnic, such games as balancing a waiter's tray of glasses of pink champagne while running sixty yards or through an obstacle course complete with hurdles. A deluxe $12,000 package includes marching bands, cheerleaders, T-shirts, and beer in baby bottles. You would be surprised at the reputedly sedate corporations using organized outings like this to raise morale among their employees.

SWAMP MEET

I read about a woman in Louisiana who earns her living doing what comes naturally. She grew up learning about the swamps and their inhabitants by tagging along with her father. The tourist commission convinced her to offer swamp tours, and sure enough, they are a success. She is a self-taught naturalist guiding her broad, flat-bottomed boat through the water hyacinths blooming on the bayou, teaching her customers about cypress trees, erosion, egrets, and oil production.

TELEPHONE

A-Dial-for-Justice.
Ever want to make a rumpus about some social injustice, a defective product, consumer fraud, but have neither the energy nor the time? There are services that spend all their time saving clients from ulcers. They will call, write, and carry the fight to the end.

How-to-Answer.
Teach employees how to answer a telephone.

Companies are very concerned with their image, and they know the first contact a consumer may have is via the telephone. Teaching telephone skills includes developing a "smiling" voice.

Busy Signal?
One secretary I know makes part of her living by trying to get through, by phone, beginning at 6:30 a.m. to a public golf course to reserve weekly golfing appointments for her clients. Continuous busy signals discourage all except determined golfers and paid dialers.

Telephone Therapy.
The latest twist in telecommunications is the call-in therapist, whereby, with the help of a credit card, it is possible to charge a consultation with a therapist.

For-profit services are an attempt to fill the gap between crisis hot lines and face-to-face therapy. It is claimed that lack of visual contact helps the client to reveal very personal problems quickly. Charges range from $15 for ten minutes to others whose fee is from $24 for 15 minutes to $60 to $90 an hour.

TELEPHONE SYSTEMS ANALYST/INSTALLER

Remember when the information operator was able to spell and could find the number you wanted; and remember when hearts raced with the excitement of A LONG DISTANCE CALL! Traditional phone companies now have competition with private companies who customize the equipment to the needs of a client. One money-making twenty-four year-old homebased operator has a buzzing enterprise all because of his early curiosity to know how a telephone worked. At twelve he was taking apart the family phone and his family LET him. Now he can support them. That's foresight.

TEXTBOOK BUYBACKS

Teachers can sell all the unsolicited textbooks that publishers send them to review. And as a college teacher I can vouch for the number of books received. (The publisher hopes for a text adoption by the teachers.) After the school library runs out of space for any more text donations, then enters the person who comes in and out of all the teachers' offices, offering anywhere from 50 cents to $10 for each of the books stacked on the desk and floor. Spring housecleaning. The distributor then sells the new books at discount prices.

TOUR LEADER

Arrange and/or conduct tours for local, out-of-state, and foreign visitors who prefer a group leader who speaks their language and knows their customs.

An unusual city tour is one from midnight to nine in the morning; another, called "the Best of Everything," which takes affluent visitors to the best shops, bars, restaurants, historical city high points; serves champagne and caviar for starters.

City walks can be organized to interesting sections such as the old quarters, wholesale flower marts, ethnic sections, and historical sites, with a stop at a colorful restaurant or bakery. A tour can be based on an architectural theme or an archaeological dig, or homes of famous personalities.

Bored conventioneers' spouses are ideal prospective customers.

Special population tours include those for teenagers, handicapped, or special interest groups. In Wyoming one-week vacations are planned for the handicapped to include overnight campouts, riding, swiming, and joining a float trip.

A "college-scouting" trip takes small groups of high school juniors and seniors on one- to six-day tours of numerous Eastern campuses.

TRAVEL AGENT/AGENCIES

Many dual careerists are travel agents. Schoolteachers seem to find this a natural, probably because they have a built-in network of clients—their colleagues.

One entrepreneur has put together a United Stated bed and breakfast directory for educators, retired or not. The idea is to offer one's home to traveling colleagues, providing a bond of common interest and a sense of security.

Make a name for yourself by specializing in some particular aspect of the travel business. Here are a few:

First Class.
These tours mean exactly what they say. They are not for the client who is down to the last million—the trip could cost that!

For Women Only.
This is a new travel specialization. Women want safety and comfort when traveling on business and pleasure and are seeking agents who understand their requirements.

Going My Way?
Travelers sometimes are looking for someone to share a ride, a cabin, a hotel room, or a meal. Putting travelers together according to similarity of backgrounds and interests is a business, called "Share-A-Trip."

Health Conscious.
There are travelers who are convinced that their annual pilgrimage to a health spa is a physical need. Tours of health spas in the United States or in Europe are quite popular.

Nonhearing Travelers.
There is an agency that features services for the deaf traveler. An interpreter is provided to make arrangements, answer questions, and generally be useful on the trip.

The Travel Nurse.
Invalid travelers can go anywhere with someone who will take care of all their needs. This agency specializes in nurses on the go.

Take-A-Guide.
Three Britishers from Take-A-Guide tour the United States to stir up business for a five-day tour of the best of Britain. The impeccably dressed (pinstripe suits, English bowlers, and carrying umbrellas) trio even furnish postcards for the folks back home. Let's go to England and beat our drum for visitors to the U.S. Dress pure American—jeans, Western boots, transistor radio earphones, and . . . a handgun?

Teen Trips.
Arranging trips for children and teenagers is a popular service for parents. The agent invites a group of parents and their children to the house to present a range of holiday options from camps to bicycling through Europe or even marine biology in the Caribbean. . . .

Swiss Chocolate Tour.
For all the chocolate lovers, this tour enables them to taste and compare the candy factories in Switzerland—a sweet-tooth delight.

TRANSCRIBER

The medical and legal professions, filmmakers, and writers have chosen to forgo the pen and push a button. Business meetings and long-distance phone meetings are taped frequently. They need you.

TRANSLATOR

Medical, engineering, and technical materials are translated into other languages. Provide written or oral communication for the non–English-speaking; be an ombudsman.

TRUCKER

A "retired" couple saved up for two trucks and book short- and long-distance hauls. They hire the drivers and find that this is a lucrative business.

TUTOR

Reading, writing, and arithmetic, foreign languages, remedial studies have become a big business. One woman has an agency employing twenty-two tutors, mostly moonlighters. An unusual aspect of her clientele is the number of whole families the tutors teach, in addition to individual instruction. This businesswoman plans to franchise.

TYPESETTER

The person who set the type for my first book was handicapped and worked from home. Typesetters have varied assignments, including résumés. It is not a difficult trade to learn.

WASHERWOMAN

When a business grosses about $7,000 a month and $2,000 is the cost for freshly washed clothing, that leaves about $5,000 monthly profit for four washerwomen. They got the bright idea of meeting the ships coming in to port, picking up the passengers' and crews' dirty laundry, and returning it the same day.

WEDDING CONSULTANT

The amount of money families spend on weddings always floors me. It's not that I am not sentimental, but the economy is so tough on newlyweds (and the rest of us) that it seems to me more sensible to give them a nest egg—cash—instead. Still, regardless of my views, the wedding business is big business. The wedding consultant does it all—from invitations to tux to place to menu to photographer. All you have to do is show up.

WIDOW COACH

First aid for widows comes in the form of a coach who helps them through the confusion of dealing with estate lawyers, medical bills, and all the unpleasant decisions needed to be made at the worst of times. Unfortunately, too many husbands think they are protecting their wives by not involving them in the day-to-day business affairs. Then, when they die, their widows are thrust into things they know nothing about. The coach I've heard about charges $35 an hour to help sort out life.

WORD PROCESSOR

Use computer technology to transform information (from written or dictated text) into letter-perfect copy. Using computer terminals, words are typed into the keyboard, viewed on the screen, and recorded on a magnetic disk simultaneously before they are printed on paper.

A Chicago bank has turned to home word-processing as an answer to the secretary shortage, letting young mothers, retirees, and the handicapped do the bank's typing in their homes via computer hookups. The computer terminal allows the employees to receive lengthy documents and other assignments at home, type them, then send back a tape to the bank, where a high-speed machine prints the copy automatically.

WORD PROFESSIONAL

Rent-a-writer. An agency that places writers or freelance writing by a word for all reasons: "creative and decorative writing" for special occasions, celebrations, holidays, and parties is someone's homebased business.

WRAPPING SERVICE

Like others, I don't mind selecting a gift, but I don't like to gift-wrap, box, and send. So I use a service.

Nasreddin Hodja, Turkey's Paul Bunyan, knelt by the sea spooning yogurt into the waves. To all the people who asked what he was doing, he said, "I am trying to change the sea into yogurt to make money." The people laughed and said it was impossible; the sea would never turn to yogurt. To which Nasreddin Hodja replied, "What if it does?"

Resources

Do your homework before you go into business. Gather as much information as you can from all the available resources, including your competition. As has been said many times before: It's a waste of time to reinvent the wheel. If you can learn a few shortcuts from someone who has already been there, why not?

However, listen with caution to what others have to say because our world could stay afloat without all of the "experts" spouting words of wisdom. Keep away from the doomsayers; you know, the ones who shake their heads negatively, who have never taken any risks in their lives.

Now is the time for the stouthearted to do detective work to ferret out information. It's impossible to list every publication that's available or crosses my desk, but the following lists will get you started. Use the library to obtain books, and save your money for the business! Use government publications from the Internal Revenue Service (IRS), the Small Business Administration (SBA), and the Department of Commerce and your state resources—remember, it's your tax dollar that pays for the publications you need.

Before the lists of related resources for specific kinds of businesses, here are the government agencies and their publications that will be of great help to you.

GOVERNMENT RESOURCES/PUBLICATIONS

Internal Revenue Service (IRS)
The staff and publications are very helpful. Some of the publications relevant to the homebaser are:

#17 Federal Income Tax
#334 Tax Guide for Small Business
#463 Travel, Gift, Entertainment Expenses
#505 Tax Withholding and Estimated Taxes
#523 Tax Information on Selling Your Home
#529 Miscellaneous Deduction
#530 Tax Information for the Home Owner
#532 Self-Improvement Tax
#583 Record-Keeping for Small Business
#587 Business Use of the Home
#900 Index to Federal Publications

Small Business Administration (SBA)
Although much of the loan assistance funds are not as available as they used to be, the publications and business advisory services, known as the Service Corps of Retired Executives (SCORE), are still ready to help you. Look under U.S. Government in the telephone directory for an office near you or write to:

SBA Publications
P.O. Box 15434
Fort Worth, TX 76119

SCORE % SBA
1441 K Street NW
Washington, D.C. 20416

Copyright Office
Library of Congress
10 First Street SE
Washington, D.C. 20540

Minority Business Development Agency
1730 K Street NW, Suite 420
Washington, D.C. 20006

American Women's Economic Development Corp.
1270 Avenue of the Americas
New York, NY 10020

The U.S. Government Printing Office
Contact the office closest to you or write for publications lists to:

The U.S. Government Printing Office
North Capitol and H Streets
Washington, D.C. 20401

PATENT/TRADEMARK/COPYRIGHT INFORMATION.

Small Business Administration—in your city or write:

SBA,
P.O. Box 15434,
Fort Worth, TX 76119.

#91. *Ideas Into Dollars.*
SSB 90. *New Product Development.*
#6.005. *Introduction to Patents.*

For Information concerning patents consult:
Commission of Patent Office
U.S. Department of Commerce
Washington, D.C. 20231

Copyright Office
% Library of Congress
Washington, D.C. 20559

U.S. Department of Agriculture and the State Departments of Commerce have local offices in your city or county. Their representatives can be of help to you.

EDUCATION—CONTINUING YOURS!

Sometimes we need more information about conducting a business or learning about a new trade or polishing up an existing skill. There are plenty of resources for you. The university system offers extension classes (generally not for credit) and community or junior colleges offer day and night classes as well. Send for their catalogs of scheduled classes.

Sometimes you may find another educational degree will get you ahead faster. Here are some books listing colleges and universities that accommodate full-time employees.

Guide to Alternative Colleges and Universities
Garrett Park Press
Garrett Park, MD 20766

*How to Get the Degree You Want: Bear's Guide to
  Non-Traditional College Degrees*
John Bear
Ten Speed Press
Box 7123
Berkeley, CA 94707

The Weekend Education Source Book
Wilbur Cross
Harper & Row
153 E. 53rd St.
New York, NY 10022

Directory of Accredited Private Home Study Schools
National Home Study Council
1601 18th Street NW
Washington, D.C. 29009

*Guide to Independent Study Through Correspondence
  Courses*
National University Extension Association
Peterson's Guides
228 Alexander Street
Princeton, NJ 08540

*The Independent Scholar's Handbook: How to Turn Your
   Interest in Any Subject into Expertise*
Ronald Gross
Addison-Wesley
Jacob Way
Reading, MA 01876

DIRECTORIES

Directory of Directories
Gale Research Company

Register of Manufacturers
(For Your State)

Better Business Bureau
(In Your State)

Dun & Bradstreet's Middle Market Directory

Dun & Bradstreet's Million Dollar Directory

The public libraries have these and many other directories.

MAGAZINES AND NEWSPAPERS—A SAMPLING

Business Week
McGraw-Hill Bldg.
1221 Avenue of the Americas
New York, NY 10020

California Business
6420 Wilshire Blvd., Suite 711
Los Angeles, CA 90048

Changing Times
The Kiplinger Washington Editors, Inc.
Editors Park, MD 20782

The Futurist
World Future Society
P.O. Box 30369
Bethesda Branch
Washington, D.C. 20014

In Business
Box 323
Emmaus, PA 18049

Money
3435 Wilshire Blvd.
Los Angeles, CA 90010

Moneysworth
251 W. 57th Street
New York, NY 10019

Venture
35 W. 45th Street
New York, NY 10036

The Wall Street Journal
200 Burnett Rd.
Chicopee, MA 01021

Working Woman
1180 Avenue of the Americas
New York, NY 10036

ASSOCIATIONS

Networking or connecting with other people in the same or different business is an excellent way to put you and your business on the map. They provide a good source for information and advice; some have newsletters, and hold monthly and national meetings.

American Woman's Economic Development Corporation
60 East 42nd St.
New York, NY 10165
212-692-9100

Start with your local Chamber of Commerce and/or a service club like Rotary or Lions. If you can't find what you want from the following list, the public library will provide the information.

American Craft Council
401 Park Avenue South
New York, NY 10016
212-696-0710

American Federation of Small Businesses
407 South Dearborn
Chicago, IL 60608
312-427-0209

American Home Sewing Council
150 West 20th Avenue
San Mateo, CA 94403
415-341-7441

American Society of Artists
1297 Merchandise Mart Plaza
Chicago, IL 60654
312-751-2500

American Yarn Spinners Association
601 W. Franklin Avenue
Box 99
Gastonia, NC 28052
704-867-7201

Apartment House Institute at New York
Community College at City University of New York
450 West 41st Street
New York, NY 10036
(for apartment house managers)

Association of Telephone Answering Services
1345 Avenue of the Americas
New York, NY 10105
212-586-4050

Association for Women in Computing, Inc.
407 Hillmoor Drive
Silver Springs, MD 20901

Center for Entrepreneurial Management
83 Spring Street
New York, NY 10012
212-925-7304

Cosmetic Career Women, Inc.
777 Seventh Avenue
New York, NY 10019

Cottage Industry Miniatures Trade Association
Box 2603
Lakewood, OH 44107

Council of Smaller Enterprises
690 Union Commerce Building
Cleveland, OH 44115
216-621-3300

Craftswomen Catalogue
2528 Milvia
Berkeley, CA 94704

Direct Selling Association
1730 M Street, Suite 610
Washington, D.C. 20036
202-293-5760

The Encyclopedia of Associations
Fifteenth edition
Gale Research Company, 1981

Farm Women
930 National Press Bldg.
Washington, D.C. 20045

Feminist Computer Technology (FCTP)
Erin Computer Systems, Inc.
4412 Jutland Drive
San Diego, CA 92117

Handweavers Guild of America
65 LaSalle Road
West Hartford, CT 06107
203-233-5124

H.O.M.E.
P.O. Box 31446
San Francisco, CA 94131

Homebased Businesswoman's Network
5 Cedar Hill Rd.
Salem, MA 01970

Home-Workers on the Move to Economic Success
(H.O.M.E.S. Guild)
31255 Cedar Valley Dr.
Westlake Village, CA 91362
818-707-0008

Independent Computer Consultants Association
P.O. Box 27412
St. Louis, MO 63141
314-567-9708

International Information/Word Processing Association
1015 North York Road
Willow Grove, PA 19090
215-657-6300

Knitting Guild of America
P.O. Box 1606
Knoxville, TN 37901

National Alliance of Home Based Business Women
P.O. Box 95
Norwood, NJ 07648

National Association for the Cottage Industry
P.O. Box 14460
Chicago, IL 60614
312-472-8116

National Association of Professional Consultants
20121 Ventura Blvd., Suite 227
Woodland Hills, CA 91364
213-703-6028

National Association for Public Continuing and
    Adult Education
1201 16th Street, NW
Washington, D.C. 20036
202-833-5486

National Association for the Self-Employed
P.O. Box 345749
Dallas, TX 75234
800-255-9226 (in Texas: 800-442-4733)

National Association of Women Business Owners (NAWBO)
2000 P Street, NW
Washington, D.C. 20036
202-338-8966

National Business League
4324 Georgia Avenue, NW
Washington, D.C. 20005
202-638-3411

National Federation of Independent Business
150 West 20th Avenue
San Mateo, CA 94403
415-341-7441

National Needlework Association
230 Fifth Avenue
New York, NY 10001
212-685-1646

National Small Business Association
1604 K Street, NW
Washington, D.C. 20006
202-296-7400

National University Extension Association
One DuPont Circle, Suite 360

Washington, D.C. 20036
202-659-3220

National Writers Club
1450 South Havana, Suite 620
Aurora, CO 80012
303-751-7844

Newsletter Association of America
1341 G Street, NW
Washington, D.C. 20045
202-347-5220

Quilter's Newsletter
P.O. Box 394
Wheat Ridge, CO 80033

Rural American Women
1522 K Street, NW, Suite 700
Washington, D.C. 20005

Rural Women Cottage Industries
505 Linder Street
Friday Harbor, WA 98250

Small Business Foundation of America
69 Hickory Drive
Waltham, MA 02154

Smaller Manufacturers Council
339 Boulevard of the Allies
Pittsburgh, PA 15222
412-391-1622

Society of Professional Journalists
840 North Lake Shore Drive, Suite 801W
Chicago, IL 60611
312-649-0060

Women in Food
Taste Unlimited
1737 Laorenzen Drive
San Jose, CA 95124

Women in Information Processing, Inc.
1000 Connecticut Ave., NW
Washington, D.C. 20036

Women's Referral Service
P.O. Box 3093
Van Nuys, CA 91407

IDEAS AND ADVICE

Briarpatch Review
330 Ellis Street
San Francisco, CA 94102

Business Use of Your Home
Publication #587
Internal Revenue Service

Dun & Bradstreet
666 Fifth Avenue
New York, NY 10019

Enterprising Women
Artemis Enterprises, Inc.
217 East 28th Street
New York, NY 10016

"The Facts for Sidelining"
In Business (April 1981).

555 Ways to Earn Extra Money
Jacy Conrad Levinson
Holt Publishing, 1982
New York, NY 10017

Federal Consumer Information Catalogue
Consumer Information Center
Pueblo, CO 81009

Give Yourself Credit #052-071-00524-2
Superintendent of Documents

U.S. Government Printing Office
Washington, D.C. 20402

Guide to Earning Extra Income
363 Seventh Avenue
New York, NY 10001

Home Business Bibliography
Small Business Administration Publications
P.O. Box 15434
Fort Worth, TX 76119

How Women Can Get Credit
National Organization for Women
425 13th Street, Suite 1048
Washington, D.C. 20004

Income Opportunities
229 Park Avenue South
New York, NY 10003

Moonlighter's Manual
Moonlight Press
611 Pawling Ave.
Troy, NY 12180

A Mother's Guide to Starting a Business at Home
Peg Hook
Harbiner House
Littleton, CO 80120

National Association of Women Business Owners
2000 P Street, NW
Washington, D.C. 20036

Networking
Mary-Scott Welch
Warner Books, 1980.
666 Fifth Ave.
New York, N.Y. 10019

New Businesses Women Can Start and Successfully Operate
Mary Leslie and David D. Seltz
Barnes & Noble, 1979
10 East 53 Street
New York, NY 10072

"*The Pleasures and Pitfalls of a Business at Home*"
In Business (August 1980).

Pricing for Small Manufacturers, #226
Small Business Administration Publications
P.O. Box 15434
Fort Worth, TX 76119

Selected U.S. Government Publications
Superintendent of Documents
U.S. Government Printing Office
Washington, D.C. 20403

Service Corps of Retired Executives (SCORE)
Free Consulting Service
Small Business Administrators
(call local office)

Small Business Reporter
Bank of America, Dept. 3120
Box 3700
San Francisco, CA 94137

Tips on Work-At-Home Schemes
Council of Better Business Bureaus, Inc.
1515 Wilson Boulevard
Arlington, VA 22209

Women's Bureau
U.S. Department of Labor
200 Constitution Avenue, NW
Washington, D.C. 20210

Worksteads
P.O. Box 29464
San Francisco, CA

SPECIFIC RESOURCES

ACCOUNTING

Accounting, Finance and Taxation: A Basic Guide for Small Business. Baker, C. Richard, and Hayes, Rick S. 1980. CBI Publishers

Accounting for Non-Accountants
Myer, John
Hawthorne Books, Inc.
New York, NY

Accounting Services for Your Small Business. Lipay, Raymond J. 1983. Ronald Press

Basic Accounting for the Small Business. 2nd ed. Cornish, Clive G. 1980. Self Counsel Press

How to Do Your Own Accounting for a Small Business. Milliron, Robert R. 1980. Enterprise Del

National Association of Accountants
919 Third Ave.
New York, NY 10022
Local chapters give free advice to small business owners.

Small-Time Operator
Kamoroff, Bernard
Bell Springs Publishing paper.

Tax Guide for Small Businesses #2334
International Revenue Service
Washington, D.C. 20403
or Local IRS Office

ADVERTISING

Advertising and Public Relations for a Small Business. Bellavance, Diane. 1982. BBA Books

Advertising and Sales Promotion. Brannen, William. 1983. Prentice-Hall 1230 Ave. of the Americas, New York, NY 10020

Advertising for the Small Business. Dean, Sandra L. 1980. Self Counsel Press

Handbook of Small Business Advertising. Anthony, Michael. 1981. Addison-Wesley Jacob Way, Reading, ME. 01867

How To Advertise: A Handbook for the Small Business. Dean, Sandra L. 1980. Enterprise Publishing Co., Inc. 725 Market Street, Wilmington, DE 19801

Profitable Advertising Techniques for Small Business. Cook, Harvey. 1981. Reston

Profitable Methods for Small Business Advertising. Gray, Ernest. 1983. Ronald Press

ANIMALS AND PETS

Cats: History, Care, Breeds
Metcalf, Christine, and George Zappler, editors, 1970.
Grosset & Dunlap, Inc.
51 Madison Ave.
New York, NY 10010

Complete Book of Dog Obedience
Saunders, Blanche, 1969.
Howell Book House
845 Third Ave.
New York, NY 10022

Dogs: Modern Grooming Techniques
Hillary Harmer, 1970
Arco Publishing Company, Inc.
219 Park Ave. South
New York, NY 10003

Dogs: Selection, Care, Training
Boorer, Wendy, 1972.
Bantam Books, Inc.
666 Fifth Ave.
New York, NY 10019

Good Dog, Bad Dog
Siegal, M., and Margolis, M. 1973
Holt Rinehart & Winston

How to Breed Dogs
Whitney, Leon, 1971.
Howell Book House
845 Third Ave.
New York, NY 10022

How to Trim, Groom & Show Your Dog
Saunders, Blanche, 1972.
Howell Book House
845 Third Ave.
New York, NY 10022

No Bad Dog
Barbara Woodhouse
Summit Books, 1982

Parakeet Breeding for Profit and Other Aviary Birds,
Glick.
Borden Publishing Company
1855 West Main St.
Alhambra, CA 91801

Understanding Your Cat,
Fox, Dr. Michael W. 1977, pap.
Bantam Books, Inc.
666 Fifth Ave.
New York, NY 10019

Understanding Your Dog
Fox, Dr. Michael W., 1972.
Coward, McCann & Geoghegan, Inc.
200 Madison Ave.
New York, NY 10016

Understanding and Training Horses
Ricci, James A. 1964.
J. B. Lippincott Company
East Washington Sq.
Philadelphia, PA 19105

ANTIQUES

Antiques: How to Identify, Buy, Sell, Refinish and Care for Them
Cole, Ann K. 1970.
David McKay Company, Inc.
119 West 40th St.
New York, NY 10018

Art & Antique Dealers League of America, Inc.
136 East 55th St.
New York, NY 10022

Basic Book of Antiques
Michael, George, 1974.
Arco Publishing Company, Inc.
219 Park Ave. South
New York, NY 10003

The Book of Pottery and Porcelain
2 vol. rev, ed. 1970.
Cox, Warren E.
Crown Publishers, Inc.
419 Fourth Ave.
New York, NY 10016

The How to Collect Anything Book: Treasure to Trivia
Dorn, Sylvia, 1976.
Doubleday & Company, Inc.
277 Park Ave.
New York, NY 10017

*Investing in Antiques and Popular Collectibles for Pleasure
and Profit*
Klamkin, Marian, and Charles Klamkin, 1975.
Funk & Wagnalls Company
% Crowell Company
666 Fifth Ave.
New York, NY 10019

Restoring Junk, Beedell, Susanne, 1971
David McKay Company, Inc.
119 West 40th St.
New York, NY 10018

ARTISAN CRAFTS

American Craft
American Craft Council
401 Park Avenue South
New York, NY 10016

The American Crafts Council
44 West 53rd Street
New York, NY 10019

Ceramics Monthly
Professional Publications, Inc.
1608 Northwest Blvd.
Columbus, OH 43212

Collectors' Guide to U.S. Auctions and Flea Markets
Susan Wasserstein
Penguin Books, 1981
625 Madison Ave.
New York, NY 10022

Craft Horizons
American Crafts Council
44 West 53rd St.
New York, NY 10019

Crafts Women's Catalogue
2528 Milvia
Berkeley, CA 94704

Creative Cash
Barbara Brabee
Artisan Crafts
P.O. Box 398
Libertyville, IL 60048

Creative Crafts
P.O. Box 700
Newton, NJ 07860

Design
1100 Waterway Boulevard
Indianapolis, IN 46202

The Goodfellow Directory of Craft Fairs
Berkley Windhover Publishers
P.O. Box 4520
Berkeley, CA 94704

Handicrafts Bibliography
Small Business Administration
P.O. Box 15434
Fort Worth, TX 76119

The Handicraft Business
Bank of America
P.O. Box 37000
San Francisco, CA 94137

How to Make Money with Your Crafts, Clark, Leta. 1973.
William Morrow & Company, Inc.
105 Madison Ave.
New York, NY 10016

How to Sell Your Artwork: A Complete Guide for Commercial and Fine Artists
Milton K. Berlye
Prentice-Hall, Inc.
Englewood Cliffs, NJ 07632

Making It Legal: A Law Primer for the Craftmaker, Visual Artist, and Writer
Davidson, Marion, and Blue, Martha
McGraw-Hill Paperbacks

Marketing Your Handicrafts
Women's Program
Massachusetts Department of Commerce and Development
100 Cambridge Street
Boston, MA 02202

Money Business: Grants and Awards for Creative Artists
The Artists Foundation, Inc.
100 Boylston St.
Boston, MA 02116

National Endowment for the Arts (Grants)
2401 E Street, NW
Washington, D.C. 20506

The New Collector's Directory
Padre Productions
Box 1275
San Luis Obispo, CA 93406

1980 Craft Worker's Market
Lapin, Lynne
Writer's Digest Books
9933 Alliance Road
Cincinnati, OH 45242

Quilter's Newsletter
P.O. Box 394
Wheat Ridge, CO 80033

Selling Your Crafts
Nelson, Norbert, 1973. pap.
Van Nostrand Reinhold Company
450 West 33rd St.
New York, NY 10001

Selling Your Handicrafts
Garrison, William, 1974
Chilton Book Company
Chilton Way
Radnor, PA 19089

Shuttle, Spindle & Dypot
Handweavers Guide of America, Inc.
998 Farmington Ave.
West Hartford, CT 06107

Small Business Administration
MA #245: "Exhibiting at Trade Shows"
SBB #1: "Handicrafts"

Women's Caucus for Art
731 44th Avenue
San Francisco, CA 93121

California Lawyers for the Arts (nonprofit organization). Offices in San Francisco, Los Angeles, and New York
Los Angeles   315 West 9th St.
                Los Angeles, CA 90015
                213-623-8311

San Francisco   Fort Mason Center
                  Building C, Room 255
                  San Francisco, CA 94123
                  415-775-7200

New York   Volunteer Lawyers for the Arts (non-profit organization)
             1285 Ave. of the Americas
             New York, N.Y. 10019
             212-977-9270

BARTER AND TRADE EXCHANGES

Barter: How to Get Almost Anything Without Money
Stapleton, Constance, and Richman, Phyllis Charles
Scribner's and Sons

International Association of Trade Exchanges (IATE)
29–48 University Terrace NW
Washington, D.C. 20016

What'll You Take for It?: Back to Barter
Prouix, Annie, Garden Way Publishing

BEAUTY

Color Me Beautiful
Carol Jackson
Ballantine Books, 1981
201 E. 50th St.
New York, NY 10022

Color, The Essence of You
Suzanne Caygill
Celestial Arts, 1980
Millbrae, CA 94030
Box 7327
Berkeley, CA 94707

Cosmetic Career Women, Inc.
777 7th Avenue
New York, NY 10019

BED AND BREAKFAST / INNS DIRECTORIES

At-Home Abroad
Sutton Town House
405 East 56th Street
New York, NY 10022

Bed and Breakfast
1205 Mariposa Avenue, #233
Miami, FL 33146

Bed and Breakfast Colorado
Box 20596
Denver, CO 80220

Bed and Breakfast in Arizona
8433 N. Black Canyon
Phoenix, AZ 85021

Bed and Breakfast Information and Sources
Box 118
Burlington, VT 05402

Bed and Breakfast International
151 Ardmore Road
Kensington, CA 94707

Bed and Breakfast League
2855 29th Street, NW
Washington, D.C. 20008

Bed and Breakfast League, Inc.
20 Nassau Street
Princeton, NJ 08540

Bed and Breakfast, NW
7707 S.W. Locust Street
Tigard, OR 97223

Classic Country Inns of America
Knapp Press
Los Angeles, CA

Colorado Dude and Guest Ranches
Box 380H
Tabernash, CO 80478

Country Inns and Back Roads
Simpson, Norman T.
Berkshire Traveller Press
Stockbridge, MA

Country Inns of the Great Lakes, Robert Morris
101 Productions, Publishers
834 Mission St.
San Francisco, CA 94103

Educators' Vacation Alternatives
317 Piedmont Rd.
Santa Barbara, CA 93105

FARMS and RANCHES DIRECTORIES
Ranch and Farm Vacations
36 East 37th Street
New York, NY 10022

Independent Innkeepers Association
% Berkshire Travelers Press
Stockbridge, MA

The Inn Book
Kathleen Neuer
Random House, Inc.
201 E. 50th St.
New York, NY 10022

Innkeeping Newsletter
P.O. Box 267
Inverness, CA 94937

International Spareroom
Box 518
Solana Beach, CA 92075

L.V. Long
317 Piedmont Road
Santa Barbara, CA 93105

Mi Casa - Su Casa B & B.
P.O. Box 950
Tempe, AZ 85281

National Bed and Breakfast Association
P.O. Box 332
Norwalk, CT 06852

Northwest Bed and Breakfast
7707 S. W. Locust
Portland, OR 97223

Ottawa Bed and Breakfast
P.O. Box 11263, Station H
Ottawa K2 #719, Canada

Rundback's Guide
RD 2, Box 355A
Greentown, PA 18426

*Start Your Own Bed & Breakfast Business—Earn Extra Cash
from Your Extra Room*
Mathews, Beverly
Pocket Books
1230 Ave. of the Americas
New York, NY 10020

Unitarian Universalist Service Committee
22907 Felbar Avenue
Torrance, CA 90505

Urban Ventures
322 Central Park West
New York, NY 10025

Sweet Dreams and Toast
P.O. Box 950
Washington, D.C. 20008

BOOKKEEPING

All About Bookkeeping: A Guide for the Small Business
Hutchinson, Susan. 1982.
Capricornus Press

Bookkeeping for Beginners
Hooper, W.E. 1970
Beekman Publishers Inc.
38 Hicks St.
Brooklyn, NY 11201

*The Computer Survival Handbook: How to Talk Back to
Your Computer*
Woolridge, Susan, and Keith London, 1973.
Educator Books, Inc.
10 North Main, Drawer 32
San Angelo, TX 76901

Data Processing for Small Businesses. SBB #80, 1977, Free. Available from nearest SBA field office.

Keeping Records in Small Business, SMA #155. 1976. Free. Available from nearest SBA field office.

Recordkeeping Systems—Small Store and Service Trade. SBB #15, Rev. 1977. Free. Available from nearest SBA field office.

Rx for Small Business Success: Accounting, Planning, and Recordkeeping Techniques for a Healthy Bottom Line
Slatter, Jeffrey. 1981.
Prentice-Hall
1230 Ave. of the Americas,
New York, NY 10020

Recordkeeping Systems—Small Store and Service Trade. SBB #15, Rev. 1977. Free. Available from nearest SBA field office.

Small Business Record Keeping
Briggaman, Joan. 1983.
Delmar Publishers, Inc.
Box 15015
Albany, N.Y. 12212-5015

CATERING

Buffet Catering
Finance, Charles.

Ahrens Publishing Company, Inc.
116 West 14th St.
New York, NY 10011

Cater from Your Kitchen
Marjorie Blanchard
Bobbs-Merrill

Catering Handbook
Weiss, Hal, and E. Weiss, 1971.
Ahrens Publishing Company, Inc.
116 West 14th St.
New York, NY 10011

Controlling and Analyzing Costs in Food Service Operations
Keiser, James, and Elmer Kallio, 1975.
Cahners Book
89 Franklin St.
Boston, MA 02110

How to Turn Your Kitchen into a Goldmine!
P.O. Box 11698
Columbia, SC 29211

Large Quantity Recipes, Terrell, Margaret, 1974.
Cahners Book
89 Franklin St.
Boston, MA 02110

Successful Catering. Splaver, Bernard R. 1975.
Cahners Book
89 Franklin St.
Boston, MA 02110

The Waiter and Waitress Training Manual, Dahmer, Sondra
J. and Kurt W. Kahl, 1975.
Cahners Book
89 Franklin St.
Boston, MA 02110

CHILDREN

(Ideas for their entrepreneurship)

Big Bucks for Kids
Leasure, Jan
Andrews and McMeel 1986

Kids Who Succeed
Feldman, Beverly Neuer
Fawcett Books 1989
201 E. 50th St.
New York, NY 10022

How to Start a Successful, Money-Making "Business" while Attending College. Goldstein, Phyllis J. 1982. Money-Maker

CLOCKS AND WATCHES

Clock Guide Identification With Prices, 2d ed
Miller, Robert W. 1975.
Wallace-Homestead Book Company
1912 Grand Ave.
Des Moines, IA 50305

Collecting and Identifying Old Clocks, Harris, Henry G. 1976.

Handbook of Watch and Clock Repair, Harris, Henry G. 1972.
Emerson Books Inc.
Reynolds Lane
Buchanan, NY 10511

The Watch Repairer's Manual, 3d ed
Fried, Henry B. 1974.
Chilton Book Company
Chilton Way
Radnor, PA 19089

COLLECTING

Acquire
170 Fifth Avenue
New York, NY 10010

Americana
381 West Center Street
Marion, OH 43302

American Antique Collector
Box 327
Ephrata, PA 17522

American Collector
Drawer C
Kermit, TX 79745

Antique Collecting
Box 327
Ephrata, PA 17522

Antique & Collectors Mart
15100 West Kellogg
Wichita, KS 67235

Antique Monthly
P.O. Drawer 2
Tuscaloosa, AL 35402

Antiques and the Arts Weekly
The Newtown Bee
Newtown, CT 06470

Antiques and Auction News
Box B
Marietta, PA 17547

The Antiques Journal
Box 1046
Dubuque, IA 52001

The Antique Press:
Florida's Newspaper of Antiques & Collectibles
P.O. Box 12047
St. Petersburg, FL 33733

Antique Toy World
The Magazine for Toy Collectors Around the World
3941 Belle Plaine
Chicago, IL 60618

The Antique Trader Weekly
P.O. Box 1050
Dubuque, IA 52001

Art & Antique Auction Review
University Arts, Inc.
IFM Building
Old Saybrook, CT 06475

Art & Antiques:
The American Magazine for Connoisseurs and Collectors
1515 Broadway
New York, NY 10036

Art & Auction
Auction Guild
250 West 57th Street
New York, NY 10019

Bay Area Collector
P.O. Box 1210
Fremont, CA 94538

Bottle News
Box 1000
Kermit, TX 79745

California Collector Antiques Investment Journal
P.O. Box 812
Carmichael, CA 95608

The Collector/Investor
740 Rush Street
Chicago, IL 60611

The Collector's Guide to U.S. Auctions and Flea Markets
Susan Wasserstein
Penguin Books, 1981

Collector's Items
Box 1275
San Luis Obispo, CA 93406

Collectors News
Box 156
Grundy Center, IA 50638

Country Americana
RD 1
Washington, NJ 07882

Early American Life
Box 1831
Harrisburg, PA 17105

The Glaze
P.O. Box 4929 G.S.
Springfield, MO 65804

Gun Week
Box 150
Sidney, OH 45365

The Jersey Devil
New Egypt Auction & Farmers Market
Route 537
New Egypt, NJ 08533

Kovels On Antiques and Collectibles:
The Confidential Newsletter for Dealers and Collectors
Antiques, Inc.
P.O. Box 22200
Beachwood, CA 44122

The Magazine Antiques
551 Fifth Avenue
New York, NY 10017

The Magazine for Collectors
1006 South Michigan Avenue
Chicago, IL 60605

Maine Antique Digest
Jefferson Street
Box 358
Waldoboro, ME 04572

Military Collectors News
Box 7582
Tulsa, OK 74105

National Antiques Review
Box 619
Portland, ME 04104

Native Arts/West
Box 31196
Billings, MN 59107

The New York Antique Almanac
of Arts, Antiques, Investments, & Yesteryear
P.O. Box 335
Lawrence, NY 11559

The New York-Pennsylvania Collector
Wolfe Publications, Inc.
4 South Main Street
Pittsford, NY 14534

Ohio Antique Review
P.O. Box 538
Worthington, OH 43085

Old Bottle Review
Box 243
Bend, OR 97701

Old Cars
Krause Publications
Iola, WI 54945

The Plate Collector
Box 1041
Kermit, TX 79745

Pottery Collectors Newsletter
Box 446
Asheville, NC 28802

Rarities:
The Magazine of Collectibles
Behn-Miller Publishers, Inc.
17337 Ventura Boulevard
Encino, CA 91316

Relics
Box 3338
Austin, TX 78764

Tri-State Trader
P.O. Box 90
Knightstown, IN 46248

West Coast Peddler
P.O. Box 4489
Downey, CA 90241

COMPUTERS

The Electronic Cottage. Deken, Joseph. 1981
Morrow
105 Madison Ave.
New York, NY 10016

Home Computers Can Make You Rich. Weisbecker, Joe.
1980. Hayden Book Company

Word Processors and Information Processing. Poynter, Dan.
1982. Para Publishing

DAY CARE

Check to see if your city regulations requires a day care
license. Some licensing agencies offer free classes.

Choosing Child Care: A Guide for Parents.
Auerback, Stevanne
New York: E. P. Dutton, 1982.
2 Park Ave.
New York, NY 10016

Come With Us to Playgroup.
Magee, Patricia B., and Ornstein, Marilyn R.
Tarrytown, NY: Prentice-Hall Media, 1981.

The Day Care Book.
Mitchell, Grace
New York: Fawcett Book Group, 1984.
201 E. 50th St.
New York, NY 10022

The Day Care Book: A Guide for Working Parents to Help Them Find the Best Possible Day Care for Their Children.
Mitchell, Grace.
Briarcliff Manor, NY: Stein & Day, 1979.
Scarborough House, Briarcliff Manor, NY 10510

Day Care: How to Plan, Develop, and Operate A Day Care Center
Belle Evans, Beth Shub, and Marlene Weinstein
Beacon Press
New York, NY

Daytime Programs for Children: Basic Goals
Children's Bureau
Department of Education
Washington, D.C. 20201

A Parent's Guide to Day Care.
Ross, Kathy G.
Summit, PA: TAB Books, 1981.
Blue Ridge Summit, PA 17214

A Parent's Guide to Day Care.
U.S. Department of Health and Human Services,
Washington, D.C.: 1981.

Quality Day Care: A Handbook for Parents and Caregivers.
Endsley, Richard C., and Bradbard, Marilyn R.
Englewood Cliffs, NJ: Spectrum Books, Prentice-Hall, 1981.
1230 Avenue of the Americas
New York, NY 10020

What Is Good Day Care?
Children's Bureau
Department of Education
Washington, D.C. 20201

Working Mothers and the Need for Child Care Service
Women's Bureau
U.S. Department of Labor
Washington, D.C. 20210

DIRECT SELLING

Direct Selling Association (DSA)
1730 M Street, NW
Washington, D.C. 20036

ELECTRIC APPLIANCES

Complete Guide to Electrical and Electronic Repairs
Grolle, Carl G. 1976.
Prentice-Hall, Inc.
Englewood Cliffs, NJ 07632

Electrical Repairs
Bernard, William. 1975. pap.
Grosset & Dunlap, Inc.
51 Madison Ave.
New York, NY 10010

Home Appliance Servicing
Anderson, Edwin P. 1974.
Theodore Audel & Company
4330 West 62d St.
Indianapolis, IN 46268

FURNITURE AND WOODWORKING

All About Antiquing and Restoring Furniture
Berger, Robert, 1971.
Hawthorn Books Inc.
260 Madison Ave.
New York, NY 10016

The Build-It Yourself Furniture Catalogue
Peterson, Franklyn N. 1976.
Prentice-Hall, Inc.
Englewood Cliffs, NJ 07632

The Furniture Maker's Handbook
Scharf, Robert, 1977.
Charles Scribner's, Sons
597 Fifth Ave.
New York, NY 10017

Woodworking and Furniture Making
Endicott, G.W., 1976, pap.
Drake Publishers, Inc.
801 Second Ave.
New York, NY 10017

GARDENS AND PLANTS

The ABC of Potted Plants
Nightingale, Gay, 1973.
Arco Publishing Company, Inc.
219 Park Ave. South
New York, NY 10003

Grow Your Own Plants
Kraner, Jack, 1973.
Charles Scribner's, Sons
597 Fifth Ave.
New York, NY 10017

Profitable Herb Growing at Home
Jacobs, Betty 1976.
Garden Way Publications
Charlotte, VT 05445

GLASS

Collecting Glass
Webber, Norman W., 1973.
Arco Publishing Company, Inc.
219 Park Ave. South
New York, NY 10003

Collector's Handbook of American Art Glass
Barrett, Richard C., 1971.
Crown Publishers, Inc.
419 Park Ave.
New York, NY 10016

How to Mend Your Treasures: Porcelain, China & Pottery,
Malone, Lawrence, 1975.
Reston Publishing Company, Inc.
% Prentice-Hall
Englewood Cliffs, NJ 07632

Wonders of Glass & Bottle Making, 2d ed
Sauzay, A., 1969
Frontier Books
% POB 805
Fort Davis, TX 79734

HISTORICAL HOUSES

Ball and Ball
463 West Lincoln Way
Exton, PA 19341

The House Emporium
199 Berkeley Place
Brooklyn, NY 11217

House Recycling
Weir, Mary
Contemporary Books, Inc.
180 N. Michigan Ave.
Chicago, IL 60601

The Old House Journal
Dept. 7
199 Berkeley Place
Brooklyn, NY 11217

Old House Journal Catalogue
69A Seventh Avenue
Brooklyn, NY 11217

Renovator's Supply
71 Northfield Road
Miller's Fall, MA 01349

Ritter & Sons, Hardware
Gualala, CA 95445

Tax Incentives for Historic Preservation
% National Trust for Historic Preservation
1785 Massachusetts Avenue, NW
Washington, D.C. 20036

HOME IMPROVEMENT AND REPAIRS

House Recycling
Weir, Mary
Contemporary Book, Inc.
180 N. Michigan Ave.
Chicago, IL 60601

How to Do Your Own Painting and Wall Papering.
Hand, Jackson, 1969. pap.
Harper & Row Publishers
49 East 33rd St.
New York, NY 10016

The Nothing Left Out Home Improvement Book
Philbin, Tom, and Fritz Koelbel. 1976.
Prentice-Hall
1230 Avenue of the Americas
New York, NY 10020

Remodelers Handbook
Williams, Benjamin. 1976. pap.
Craftsman Book Company
542 Stevens Ave.
Solana Beach, CA 92075

IMPORT/EXPORT

American Importers Association
420 Lexington Avenue
New York, NY 10017

An Introduction to Doing Import and Export Business
Chamber of Commerce of the U.S.
1615 H Street, NW
Washington, D.C. 20062

Basic Guide to Exporting
U.S. Government Printing Office
Washington, D.C. 20402

Foreign Trade Marketplace
Gale Research Company
Book Tower
Detroit, MI 48226

How to Be an Importer and Pay for Your World Travel
Mary Green and Stanley Gilmar
Mary Green Enterprises
319 Grant Ave.
San Francisco, CA 94108

231

How to Prepare and Process Export-Import Documents: A Fully Illustrated Guide.
Hicks, Tyler G. 1983.
International Wealth Success
Box 186
Merrick, NY 11566

Import/Export
Small Business Administration
P.O. Box 15434
Fort Worth, TX 76119

Importing into the U.S.
U.S. Customs Service
Superintendent of Documents
U.S. Printing Office
Washington, D.C. 20402

Trade Channel Publications
One World Trade Center
Suite 86013
New York, NY 10048

Trade Directories of the World
Croner Publications
Queen's Village, NY 11428

U.S. Department of Commerce
Washington, D.C. 20233

INVENTIONS (SEE PATENTS.)

American Inventor
10310 Menhart Lane
Cupertino, CA 95014

Commission of Patent Office
U.S. Department of Commerce
Washington, D.C. 20231

Complete Guide to Making Money With Your Ideas and Inventions,
Richard E. Paige 1973.
Prentice-Hall
Englewood Cliffs, NJ 07632

The Innovation Millionaires: How They Succeed
Charles Scribner's Sons
115 Fifth Ave.
New York, NY 10003

International New Products Newsletter
Box 191
Back Bay Annex
Boston, MA 02117

Inventing For Fun and Profit
Robert L. Hallock
Crown Publishers, Inc.
225 Park Ave. South
New York, NY 10003

Inventor's Handbook. Fenner, T. W., and Everett, J. L.
Chemical Publishing Company, Inc.
200 Park Ave.
New York, NY 10003

New Products and Processes
Newsweek International
P.O. Box 424
Livingston, NJ 07039

Product Design and Development
Chilton Company
Chilton Way
Radnor, PA 19089

Venture Capital
Capital Publishing Co.
Box 348
Wellesley Hill, ME 02181

JEWELRY

The Jewelry Engraver's Manual
Hardy, Allen R. 1976, pap.
Modern Jewelry: Design & Technique
Brynner, Irena, 1976, pap.
Working with Copper, Silver & Enamel
Sjoberg, Jan and Ove Sjoberg, 1974, pap.
Van Nostrand Reinhold Company
450 West 33rd St.
New York, NY 10001

LAMPS AND SHADES

How to Make Lampshades and Draperies
Montagana, Pier, pap.
147 McKinley Ave.
Bridgeport, CT 06606

Lampmaking
Murphy, Bruce, 1976.
Drake Publishers, Inc.
801 Second Ave.
New York, NY 10017

MAIL ORDER

The American Mail Order Business & How to Succeed in it
Sparks, Howard, 1966.
Frederick Fell, Inc.
389 Park Ave. South
New York, NY 10016
2131 Hollywood Blvd.
Hollywood, FL 33020

Associated Third-Class Mail Users
1725 K St. NW
Washington, D.C. 20006

Direct Mail Marketing Association
1730 K St. NW
Washington, D.C. 20006

How Mail Order Fortunes Are Made
Stein, Alfred
Arco Publishing Co., 1977
219 Park Ave. South
New York, NY 10033

How to Start and Operate a Mail Order Business
Simon, Julian S.
McGraw-Hill, 1976
1221 Avenue of the Americas
New York, NY 10020

How to Start and Run a Successful Mail Order Business,
Martyn, Sean, 1971.
David McKay Company, Inc.
119 West 40th St.
New York, NY 10018

Mail Advertising Service Association International
7315 Wisconsin Ave.
Bethesda, MD 20014

Mail Order Association of America
P.O. Box 7074
Alexandria, VA 22307

Mail Order Enterprises
Small Business Reporter
Bank of America, Dept. 3120
P.O. Box 37000
San Francisco, CA 94137

Mail Order Moonlighting
Hoge, Cecil C., Sr.
Ten Speed Press, 1976
Box 7123
Berkeley, CA 94707

National Mailing List Houses,
SBB #29, 1977.
Free from nearest SBA field office or write to:
Small Business and Administration
Washington, D.C. 20416

National Zip Code Directory
Directory of Post Offices
International Mail
Postal Bulletin

Selling by Mail Order,
SBB #3, 1977.
Free from nearest SBA field office or write to:
Small Business and Administration
Washington, D.C. 20416

Superintendent of Documents
Postal Service
Washington, D.C. 20260

MINIATURES

Inside the World of Miniatures and Dollhouses: A Comprehensive Guide to Collecting and Creating
Rosner, Bernard, and Jay Beckerman, 1976.
David McKay Company, Inc.
750 Third Ave.
New York, NY 10017

Making Miniatures: How To Make Them, Use Them, Sell Them
Meras, Phyllis, 1976.
Houghton Mifflin Company
2 Park St.
Boston, MA 02107

NEWSLETTERS

Direct Marketing—Home Communicator
224 Seventh Street
Garden City, NY 11532

Newsletter Association of America
14 East Jackson Blvd.
Chicago, IL 60604

Newsletter of Newsletters
41 West Market Street
Rhinebeck, NY 12572

PAINTING

Drawing and Painting
Knight, S.A. 1974, pap.
David McKay Company, Inc.
750 Third Ave.
New York, NY 10017

Painting: A Creative Approach, Guide to Modern Methods and Materials,
2d ed, Colquhoun, Norman, 1969.
Peter Smith Publishers
6 Lexington Ave.
Magnolia, MA 01930

The Restorer's Handbook of Easel Painting
Emile-Male, Gilbert. 1976.
Van Nostrand Reinhold Company
450 West 33rd St.
New York, NY 10001

PARTY ENTERTAINERS

The Art of Juggling
Benge, Ken, 1977
Box 366
Mountain View, CA 94042

M-U-M Publication
The Society of American Magicians
4110 W. 109th St.
Oak Lawn, IL 60453

Puppertry Journal
Puppeteer of America, Inc.
Box 1061
Ojai, CA 93023

PHOTOGRAPHY

Basic Black and White Photography, Rehm, Karl M. 1976.
Cash from Your Camera, Peek.
Getting Started in Photography, Barry, Les. 1975.
Where and How to Sell Your Pictures at a Profit, Bennett,
E. and R. Maschke, 1971.
American Photographic Book Publishing Company
750 Zeckendorf Blvd.
Garden City, NY 11530

How to be a Freelance Photographer
Schwartz, Ted. 1980.
Contemporary Books, Inc.
180 N. Michigan
Chicago, IL 60601

PICTURE FRAMING

A Complete Do-It-Yourself Guide to Picture Framing
Duren, Lista, 1976.
Houghton Mifflin Company
2 Park St.
Boston, MA 02107

The Frame Book
Newman, Thelma, 1974.
Crown Publishing, Inc.
419 Fourth Ave.
New York, NY 10016

PUBLISHING/WRITING

American Booksellers Association
122 E. 42nd St.
New York, NY 10017

Association of American Publishers
One Park Ave.
New York, NY 10016

The Authors Guild, Inc.
234 W. 44th St.
New York, NY 10036

The Book Market: How To Write, Publish and Market Your Book
Mathieu, Aron
Andover Press, Inc.
516 W. 34th St.
New York, NY 10001

Books: From Writer to Reader
Greenfield, Howard
Crown Publishers, Inc.
One Park Ave.
New York, NY 10016

How To Get Happily Published: A Complete and Candid Guide
Appelbaum, Judith, and Nancy Evans, 1982.
New American Library
1633 Broadway
New York, NY 10019

How to Make Money in Your Spare Time by Writing
Edited by Kirk Polking, 1971.

Law and the Writer
Polking, Kirk, and Leonard S. Meranus
Writer's Digest Books
1507 Dana Ave.
Cincinnati, OH 45207

What You Aren't Supposed to Know About Writing and Publishing
Schwartz, Laurens R.
Shapolsky Publishers, Inc.
136 West 22nd St.
New York, NY 10011

Writer's Market '77
Edited by Jane Koester and Paula Arnett Sandhage, 1977.
Writer's Digest
9933 Alliance Rd.
Cincinnati, OH 45242

Writer's Market: Where To Sell What You Write
Writer's Digest Books
9933 Alliance Rd.
Cincinnati, OH 45242

Writing Juvenile Stories and Novels
Whitney, Phillis A. 1976.
Writers, Inc.
8 Arlington St.
Boston, MA 02116

ROADSIDE MARKETS

Cash From Your Garden, Roadside Farm Stand
Lynch, David, 1976, pap.
Garden Way Publishing Company
Charlotte, VT 05445

Marketing Perishable Food Products
Adams, Arthur B. 1969.
AMS Press, Inc.
56 East 13th St.
New York, NY 10003

STAMPS AND COINS

Appraising and Selling Your Coins, 5th ed.
Friedlberg, Robert, and Jack Friedberg, 1971.
Coin and Currency Institute, Inc.
393 Seventh Ave.
New York, NY 10001

Fell's Official Stamp Guide
Burns, Franklin R.
Frederick Fell, Inc.
389 Park Ave. South
New York, NY 10016

Scott's Stamp Catalogue, Vols. I–IV.
Scott Publishing Company
10102 F Street
Omaha, NE 68127

Associations concerned with stamps and coins are:

American Numismatic Association
818 Cascade
Colorado Springs, CO 80903

American Philatelic Society
P.O. Box 800
State College, PA 16801
Publishes *The American Philatelist*, Monthly

American Stamp Dealers Association
147 West 42nd St.
New York, NY 10036

Society of Philatelic Americans
P.O. Box 9086
Cincinnati, OH 45209

TOYS

Creative Soft Toy Making
Peqke, Pamela, 1974.
Bobbs-Merrill Company, Inc.
1430 62nd St.
Indianapolis, IN 46268

American Folk Toys: How to Make Them
Schnacke, Dick, 1974, pap.
Penguin Books, Inc.
625 Madison Ave.
New York, NY 10022

Soft Toys for Fun and Profit
Bertrand, Mary, 1974
A.H. & A.W. Reed Books
Rutland, VT 05701

Price Guide to Dolls
Miller, Robert W. 1976.
Price Guide to Toys
Miller, Robert W. 1976.
Wallace-Homestead Book Company
1912 Grand Ave.
Des Moines, IA 50305

TYPING/SECRETARIAL SERVICES

How to Earn $25,000 a Year or More Typing at Home
Drouillard, Ann and William Keefe, 1973.
Frederick Fell, Inc.
386 Park Ave. South
New York, NY 10016

How to Set Up and Run a Successful Typing Service
Goodrich, Donna. 1982. Wiley

How to Start a Profitable Typing Service at Home
Montaperto, Nicki. 1981.
Barnes & Noble

How to Start and Run a Successful Home Typing Service
Glenn, Peggy, 1980.
Aames-Allen Publishing Co.
Huntington Beach, CA 92648

How to Start Your Own Secretarial Services Business at Home
Kozlow, S.G. 1980.
SK Publications

Starting Your Own Secretarial Business
Betty Lonngren and Gloria Shoff
Contemporary Books
180 N. Michigan Ave.
Chicago, IL 60601

What's Your Business?

Send to: Beverly Neuer Feldman, Ed.D.
           P.O. Box 27816
           Los Angeles, CA 90027

The following homebased businesses should be added to the next edition and featured in the newsletter:

_____

_____

_____

_____

_____

_____

_____

_____

_____

COMPANY NAME

_____

YOUR NAME

_____

STREET ADDRESS

_____

CITY   STATE   ZIP

_____

TELEPHONE: area code and number

ABOUT THE AUTHOR

Beverly Neuer Feldman, Ed. D., is a nationally known career/education/homebased-business consultant and teaches at Los Angeles Valley College and holds seminars at universities and colleges throughout the country. She has a Master of Arts degree in Human Development and a Doctorate in Education. Dr. Neuer Feldman has written several bestselling career books, appears frequently on television and radio, and has several homebased businesses of her own.

Known as ''the work doctor'' in her newspaper and magazine articles, she successfully practices what she believes others can learn to do: financial self-defense, diversification for an assured income, and a way to work that provides adventure, pleasure, and fun.